SHAKE THE CITY:
Experiments in Space and Time, Music and Crisis

Alexander Billet

1968 Press

First published in 2022 by 1968 Press

ISBN: 978-1-9196019-3-9 (pbk & ebk)

1968 Press
London

*To Neil Davidson: an incomparable thinker,
militant, and music lover.
We miss you.*

Acknowledgements

The initial idea for this book came about in 2012, more than a decade before what you're holding in your hands. For years, it was nothing but an inkling, vaporware for cultural criticism, weaving its way through various iterations as I discovered more artists, more theory, and as unfolding events made its argument clearer. What made all of this into something more was years of encouragement from friends and loved ones, colleagues and comrades. These are the people who, despite my own self-deprecation, insisted that I had something important to say.

I had no idea what to expect during my first book. Having a team willing to hold my hand a bit really helped. To everyone at 1968 Press – Jaice Titus, Izzy Dann, and Dan Bristow – you've shown me all the love and engagement that a first-time book author wants – and, quite frankly, needs – from their publisher.

To Steven "Dad" Billet, Jon Danforth-Appell, Hector Rivera, and Boris Dralyuk for reading early chapter drafts and book proposals. Thank you for your indulgence and feedback. Also, to my long-suffering Kickstarter supporters, who handed their money over to me when I hadn't written more than a handful of successful articles, then waited a decade while I taught myself how to write a book. I sincerely hope that wait was worth it.

The combination of music with psychogeography creates a quizzical nexus, and even those of us fascinated with it aren't sure if we're onto something or if it's just a bunch of fantastical bullshit rattling round our fevered skulls. Having accomplished thinkers give you the initial push – sometimes people with prestigious initials after their names, sometimes people who have just put in the sweat, the work, and the thought – can be crucial. I therefore simply must mention the crew in and around Historical Materialism I have been lucky enough to get to know over these past several years. The list is fairly long: Jaz Blackwell-Pal, Paul Reynolds, Richard Seymour, Neil Davidson (RIP), Jamie Allinson, Rosie Warren, Crystal Stella Becerril, Jonny Jones, Anindya Bhattacharya, Neil Rogall, David Renton, Sebastian Budgen (get back to work…), Elia El Khazen, Joe Sabatini, Holly Lewis, Jonas Marvin, Steve Edwards, Toby Manning, Jordy Cummings. Thanks to all of you.

It would be remiss of me to leave out Olivia Mansfield and Arjun Mahadevan, who gave me a crash course in grime one drunken night at their flat in Streatham. The same must be said for Katy Fox-Hodess, Francisco Núñez Capriles, and Francisca Moraga who helped me filling my own gaps regarding music and resistance in contemporary Chile. The insights all of them provided ended up opening a whole new layer of research that made this book infinitely stronger.

To the Locust Arts & Letters Collective – Adam Turl, Tish Turl, Mike Linaweaver, Leslie Lea, Laura Fair-Schulz, Drew Franzblau, Adam Ray Adkins, Omnia Sol, Anupam Roy, and Richard Hamilton – for just being a brilliant gathering of artists, writers, and comrades. I am privileged to work with all of you.

Finally, to my brilliant and beautiful partner, Kelsey Goldberg: for putting up with my long and aimless yarns about music theory and psychogeography, for helping me make my purple prose a bit more intelligible, for not letting me give up when I was at my most discouraged. You haven't just made this book better, you've made me better.

CONTENTS

Opening Notes
An Introduction   i

Part One
Songs in an Alien City   1

Part Two
Survival Rhythms   31

Part Three
Anachronism, Attack   61

Part Four
Revolt Against Exterminism: A Coda   91

Part Five
Shake the City Playlist   123

Opening Notes
An Introduction

Nobody can dismiss the role that music plays in daily life. The love and excitement our favorite songs stir in us are proof. Music impacts us in ways we find difficult to describe. If any of us were asked to picture our lives without it, we would be flummoxed. Such an existence would be either indescribably dismal or simply indescribable. We don't just "enjoy" music. We are *moved* by it.

This same ineffability is makes music's social function so difficult to understand. What is music *for*? What *purpose* does it serve in this thing called life? These may be dry, prosaic questions to ask, but over the years, I find myself obsessed with them.

This book is an attempt to find answers. In writing it I've taken two arguments as given. The first is that music – its effect on our bodies and minds and emotional states – allows us to feel something greater than the sum of our parts, to imagine our lives as magnificent and fulfilling. The second is that the world around us is telling us the opposite, that life is an increasingly torturous journey from one hard scrabble to the next.

We don't need to look hard for evidence of the second argument. The world often feels increasingly bleak. The slide toward authoritarianism and toxic nationalisms;

a sharp decline in living standards (across the board but especially for young people); climate catastrophe that threatens the very fabric of society; and of course, the added specter of global pandemic; these all contribute to a precarious existence that feels, increasingly, futureless.

As for the first argument, it merits some unpacking. In the face of this moment in history, it is tempting to view our favorite music – along with our favorite films, paintings, books or TV shows – as an escape, a balm, a reprieve from the anxieties of the world. I can't argue with this. But the nature of "escape" deserves interrogation.

Too often, this label of escapism is its own dismissal, compartmentalizing art and culture away from a more serious reality. Sometimes, accusations of escapism are thinly veiled as a riposte, insisting that the world really isn't that bad and we should stop moaning. More often it's a condescending pat on the head, a suggestion that for as much as we might enjoy our imaginations, we must remember that they have little to no bearing on the real world.

This dismissal reaches into the realm of daily life's design, to such a degree that it feels like knee-jerk common sense. For the past four decades, the idea of art as a public right has been thoroughly undermined through a real, material assault on public life. In 2012, the Chicago Teachers Union saw that arts education in their city's schools had been so defunded that the union put its restoration near the beginning of its pamphlet in the run-up to teachers' contract negotiations and subsequent strike. Noting that it is typically the poorest schools, disproportionately in neighborhoods of color, that have their arts and music teachers cut, the CTU pamphlet also pointed to studies that showed children with arts education have greater self-awareness and empathy, are more enthusiastic about learning, have stronger critical thinking skills, and are more likely to form "unique and unusual ideas."[1]

It bears asking why, exactly, administrators of basic education might see such thinking as unnecessary for poor and working-class students. The answer is that as standardized tests encourage students to memorize and regurgitate by rote, better preparing them for menial, repetitive tasks, the option to think past the confines of "the real" become at best a complication, and at worst a threat.

Thus the imagination isn't just diminished in schools. It is diminished in the shuttering of free and accessible art studios or rehearsal spaces, the conflation of talent with celebrity, and the dominant acceptance that only the truly "gifted" (read: wealthy and connected) have the right to unlimited creativity. The neoliberal imagination is literally impoverished. This is, ultimately, deliberate. I want to challenge this impoverishment, and the commonsense dismissal accompanying it. Without imagination, without the big "what if?", nothing would exist in the way of human achievement. It's just as true for the individual as it is for the masses, and nobody's imagination is undervalued quite like that of the masses.

Denial of this mass imaginary is a cornerstone of what we have come to call "capitalist realism," the ideology by which capitalism has convinced us that it is truly the only option for a society. Most of modern history has seen grand egalitarian visions compete for the allegiance of millions. These different worlds, these alternative futures, have inspired us to fight, sometimes to die, for the possibility of something better. The assault on

---

[1] Chicago Teachers Union, 'The Schools Chicago's Students Deserve', (2012), https://www.ctulocal1.org/blog-img/text/SCSD_Report-02-16-2012-1.pdf.

and privatization of public life has severed this dialectic. Powerful nay-sayers easily brush aside visions for a fundamentally different way of life as "utopian." But at a time when dystopia is so unbearably ever-present, so over-weaning and unavoidable, can we afford to so easily relinquish the utopian?

This book answers that question with an emphatic "no." It declares that there is still a utopian narrative to be claimed and reinvigorated. Doing so cannot be an afterthought for a strategy of radical transformation, dismissed like we have been taught to do with the human imagination. No, the utopian imaginary *must be at the center* of that strategy. To show people that another world is conceivable is *a priori* essential to making it possible.

In formulating this argument, there several radical cultural writers and thinkers who have proven essential. The most obvious is Mark Fisher, whose shadow looms large over this book, as it does over left cultural theory in general. It was Fisher who gave us the term capitalist realism, and whose passing came just as he begun to theorize its antidote of "acid communism," a liberatory framework in which the socio-political and cultural-aesthetic are unified under a banner of everyday radical democracy. A promise of a world in which everyone has the resources to reach their full creative potential, it is intended as a catalyst toward a fundamental transformation of human subjectivity.

In some ways, this book is an attempt to map one potential acid communist path out of capitalist realism. The use of a wide array of critical and cultural theory – from the Frankfurt School to the Situationists, Henri Lefebvre to Frantz Fanon, from the blues theory of Amiri Baraka to the abolitionist geographies of Ruth Wilson Gilmore – flow from this mandate. All have an essential role to play. At the other end, hopefully, is a vision for a world in which collective imagination is realized in the shape and form of daily life.

All the creative arts play a role in sensitizing us to this world. All of them are unique in their contribution. I would argue that music's role is especially difficult to define because it works on our senses and psyches in a particularly deep way. Rather than delivering the vision of a different world ready-made to us like, say, a painting or film might do, music requires time for its effects on us to unfold. Its rhythms and arrangements of notes prompt our minds and emotions to feel a different mode of existence, to view the change in sensation as an invitation to imagine. If it seizes our attention with enough strength, it literally provokes *movement* out of us, anything from tapping the foot and humming to wild dancing and singing at the top of our lungs.

I have chosen the city as my primary site of inquiry for a few related reasons. Cities and music are inextricably bound together. Their conglomeration of people, resources, and ideas have given rise to popular music as we understand and experience it. Even sounds and genres that have originated in primarily rural settings – genres like, say, the delta blues – have only been able to spread and influence musicians around the globe due to the industrialization that has flowed out of urban areas. This fosters a tension that can be found in virtually any musical genre. Styles collide, giving rise to new subgenres and scenes, to all manner of contradictions concerning race, class, sexuality, gender, and nation. It is at turns problematic and thrilling, holding equal potentials for erasure and connection across lines of difference.

These possibilities are inevitably shaped by the environment in which music is made and experienced. This is something often sidestepped by those who would dismiss popular culture as a frivolous escape. How we interpret a song, the alternate worlds we find within it, has so much to do with the worlds already on offer to us. While the contemporary city does indeed offer possibility for alterity, of an otherness that we may find more appealing and suitable for a life worth living, these possibilities have been severely curtailed by the way the city itself has been shaped.

Late capitalism's contours – its replacement of collective narrative and social responsibility with the sacred individual – finds echo in the city's shape. Its privatization of public space, its increasing reliance on heavy-handed and often deadly policing, its de facto racial segregation and overall alienation; these enforce on us the infeasibility of an alternative.

As I argue in the first chapter, these same contours are brought to bear on popular music. As public access to the arts diminishes (indeed, in the United States it is nearly non-existent), artists and listeners alike are forced to rely on private enterprise. How this affects music has been the complaint of artists and fans for as long as there has been a music industry; from the systematic shortchanging of Black jazz musicians by white-owned record labels to the blackballing of certain songs on American radio after the September 11th terror attacks.

Despite dramatic changes to the way music is distributed and listened to over the past two decades, the profit motive remains primary. The rise of streaming services on mobile devices has atomized our listening experience. Services can now tailor what we hear to our liking, what is suggested to us after the end of an album or song. But like many aspects of daily consumer life that claim to value "freedom of choice," there is also a profoundly manipulative dimension to the programs and algorithms, narrowing the scope within any given genre or style. Consequently, as I also mention in the first chapter, recording artists themselves are pressured to write material that better conforms to streaming services' ideas of what sounds like something else, of what is more likely to receive higher exposure. The range of possibility is constrained, the other worlds within music diminish.

Does this mean that music's utopian dimension is snuffed out? Not entirely. But if it is to play a utopian role then we must name these obstacles – physical, psychological, technological – for what they are. Furthermore, we must give the idea and hope of utopia space to expand.

Of course, music cannot literally "change the world" any more than a painting's subject can walk out of frame and shake hands with us. But music's invocation of time allows us to feel a pace of life that may conflict with the arrangement of the world around us.

Geographers look at space through analytic scales: the global, the regional, the national, the local. Radicals and feminists have both argued that geographic analysis – of contradictions, inequities, changeabilities – can also be applied on more granular scales to the neighborhood and domestic sphere. Throughout this book, I will be looking at the production of space – and, for that matter, time – on all these levels, often moving quickly from one to another. The ramifications of events on one scale also impact how life is experienced elsewhere on the scales. Wars produce political and military decisions on regional scales that have consequences for how safe a family might feel in their community, even whether they have a community or home at all. They also frequently disrupt the international distribution of food and resources, changing the way working people behave in cities half a world away. Conversely, uprisings from below, movements of actual people, can create crises for governments well beyond a single set of borders.

It's here that we must return to the concept of *movement*, of the way music impels us to move, and the way in which this movement intersects with renewed, incendiary approaches to space. It is not for nothing that we call insurgencies of new ideas – be they in music or in the socio-political realm – movements. In both cases it denotes not just a shift, but a shift provoked through agency, a pushing aside of old conventions by those who insist things could be done differently.

For this reason, the denial of music and the space to create it is a frequent feature of history. It may be through direct repression or censorship or, as in our own time, a matter of hegemony and manufactured consent, but it is an unavoidable part of maintaining power going back centuries.

The Greek philosopher Plato, writing two thousand years before anyone dreamed of recorded sound, passionately warned Athens' rulers against allowing slaves access to music in *The Republic:* "When modes of music change," he wrote, "the fundamental laws of the state change with them." Or, in the vulgarized version: "When the mode of music changes, the walls of the city shake."[2]

Music as a threat. Not metaphorically. Not the stuff of vague and sentimental slogans, but as a component of ungovernability, bringing to life the friction between space and time, being and becoming.

The remaining chapters of this book are dedicated to understanding this process, and how these two different understandings of movement intersect given the current social, political, and economic environment. Social atomization takes its toll on all of us, particularly in oppressed communities subject to racial and ethnic segregation,

---

2 See Plato, *The Republic;* accessible online: https://www.gutenberg.org/files/1497/1497-h/1497-h.htm

which persists on an economic basis despite its elimination at the legal level in almost every country. The second chapter of this book examines how, as both music and the city continue to engender these oppressive modes, artists and listeners in even the most disaffected areas manage to find subjectivity in music that runs counter to their social domination. This can be done through the creation of new music, or through redefinition of songs that already exist, reinterpreting them in such a way that emphasizes their power and potential as fully realized human beings capable of controlling their own lives.

The third chapter looks at what happens when this process collectivizes. What I mean by this is what happens when the oppressed, the exploited and alienated, find each other and construct a common vision through music. This does not always necessarily take place in a political context. The rave and EDM scenes of the 1980s and 90s did not originate on explicitly political terms. But the repression these scenes faced from governments hellbent on controlling space, and the multiracial complexion of these scenes, put them on a collision course with police and politicians who sought to shut down dance parties.

There is an affinity between these musical movements and the way in which powerful social movements often incorporate music. In both cases, there is a reach toward the utopian, an attempt to transform space with music, often counter to that space's intended use. It has been on display in the "grime rebellion" that emerged from the 2010 student uprising in Britain, in the relationship of hip-hop to Black Lives Matter, and in the stunning ways in which song has been deployed in recent uprisings in Lebanon, Haiti, Chile and France. Public spaces that before aimed to siphon the public along paths of acceptability are reconfigured as spaces of freedom and futurity.

The book's final chapter asks, honestly and without offering any easy answers, what the current prospects are for this kind of futurity to find its bearings. *Shake the City* is being written at a heady time. The Covid-19 pandemic has changed public life and politics as we know them, which is to say nothing of the real-life climate crisis. The jury is still out on whether this spurs late capitalism to leave the neoliberal model behind, finally rediscovering the necessity for at least a modicum of permanent public investment.

Far more troubling is how the pandemic has entrenched and accelerated the rise of the far-right in governments and streets around the world. Capitalism now bares its teeth, unleashing a nasty impulse that revels in human suffering and mass death. Police are cheered with impunity for brutalizing people of color and immigrants. Open attacks on trans and queer people ramp up. Elected leaders encourage vigilante violence. Middle-class business owners openly demand we "sacrifice the weak" for their massive houses and country clubs.

On the other end of the polarization, the resurgence of far-left continues, though far less dramatically. It has suffered the crushing defeats in recent years – the unraveling of the Sanders and Corbyn projects, bills and laws criminalizing protest – but the realization that the center cannot hold is deepening. Socialism, however it is defined, continues to grow in popularity among young people. The popular uprisings that were interrupted by Covid, against privatization, authoritarianism, inequality, are again beginning to stir. The refrain of socialists for over a century, a choice between "socialism or barbarism," is made strikingly literal.

What this means for our right to the city, to a decent life, to music and art and human creativity, is very much an open question. It is not a frivolous one, though.

OPENING NOTES

Not even in such a bleak world. In fact, precisely because things seem so bleak, we cannot afford to not ask these questions. Our ability to imagine a different future, even as the right formulates and enacts its own dystopia in real time, is more urgent than ever.

In essence, *Shake the City* is a call for us to reconnect with an imaginary buried and obscured under the detritus of repression and catastrophe. It insists that our lives can in fact be the magnificent and fulfilling experiences we glimpse when we are gripped by music and art. Against the torpor of authoritarianism and apocalypse, we must nurture any opportunity to dream of a future worth living.

Part One
Songs in an Alien City

> "The reigning economic system is a vicious circle of isolation. Its technologies are based on isolation, and they contribute to that same isolation. From automobiles to television, the goods that the spectacular system chooses to produce also serve it as weapons for constantly reinforcing the conditions that engender 'lonely crowds.'"
> Guy Debord, *Society of the Spectacle*

> "You got a heart of glass or a heart of stone
> Just you wait 'til I get you home
> We've got no future, we've got no past
> Here today, built to last
> In every city, in every nation
> From Lake Geneva to the Finland Station"
> Pet Shop Boys, 'West End Girls'

Asocial listening in an asocial world

Before you go outside, you put your ear buds in. By now it's become second nature, unthinking and perfunctory. The world you curate into your ears is far more bearable than the one on the other side of that front door. Perhaps you're one of the (un)lucky few with a car, taking it to and from work each day. Or, (un)luckier yet, you have no place to go. So you stay inside. But be it the car or the tiny bedroom, you can control that environment. The music you choose is part of that control.

It is futile to act as if we can carry that same kind of control to the outside, but we are trying harder than ever. Walking to public transport, to work, to school, the store, we listen not to engage and connect, but to ignore.

And who can blame us? What greets us on that outside? Others trying just as hard as to ignore us. Casting our gaze up, we are reminded who rules the skyline. Those inside the glass and concrete monstrosities that dominate it can forget that they are in a fortress because the fortress is not for them. It is for us, outside. We don't dare try to enter, mostly because it has so eternally towered over us that the very notion has never occurred to us. Even if it only went up last week, it floats with impunity.

Inevitably, our gaze floats back down, and we are reminded of the havoc this skyline has wrought. We catch it in brief flashes. Streets and sidewalks intended to usher us along without patience or contemplation, and with plenty of cops reminding us should we forget. Stores we can't afford, restaurants we can't afford. Apartments we can't afford, soon to be torn down and turned into condominiums that laugh at the very notion of affordability. Humble bars, independent venues and other favorite haunts shuttered, their memories now only in our head. Public parks or squares neglected or so tightly restricted that even the thought of relaxing in them makes us nervous.

As for those like us, the Others making their isolated way through the space, we rarely think of them as an "us." More often, they are obstacles, impediments, "in the way" of a destination we aren't particularly excited to get to. They aren't friends or neighbors or other residents. If they are unhoused, they are barely considered human beings.

Who wouldn't want to shut out this world? We can't fully ignore it; our eyes won't let us. But at least we can use our ears to make it numb. The rhythms and sounds curated by (or, increasingly, for us) are a ready-made world far more in line with our wishes and desires. The frustration you feel for a slow-moving human in your way is softened by the dulcet sounds of your wedding song. Headlines of disaster glanced at the newsagent melt away in favor of a jaunty new single from your favorite dance pop artist. The anxiety of a growing tent encampment on the sidewalk can be processed emotionally by switching to your "angry playlist." The environment in which we live, work, and occasionally play is not shaped for us. Our music can make it *feel* like it is. Or at least that's what we tell ourselves.

The ubiquity of headphones signifies the ever-tightening grip of capitalist time. This is a mode of time experienced, in its truest form, as the atomized individual. Now, more than ever, music is experienced individually rather than collectively. Even surrounded by others, we are alone.

This was not always the case. For most of history, music was, by necessity, something in the open air. Even the lone hermit humming to themselves was liable to have their tune heard by passersby. The idea of privatized music, sound hoarded solely for individual enjoyment, is relatively new.

We can trace its rise through the history of recorded sound. This evolution reflects the increasing sophistication of capitalism's productive capacities, and with it, the transformation of musical expression and cultural consumption. Before musical instruments and sheet music were widely available, we packed into concert halls or gathered in town squares to hear music. We shared sound and rhythm with other people. We acknowledged and embraced each other. We sang, we clapped, we danced.

Music in the domestic space was not unheard of, or even uncommon. But the industrial production of musical instruments and sheet music increased its spread. The concert halls and live music persisted, were still popular. Nonetheless, the die had been cast.

With the advent of Edison's phonograph, this dimension became more deeply engrained, accelerated by the rise of radio. It was (and is) inarguably marvelous. For the first time ever, we could hear sound being made before us that was *not actually being made in front of us*. We could pick and choose regardless of whatever musical skills we may or may not have. As wax cylinders gave way to vinyl records, the phenomenon became ever more a part of everyday life.

After the Second World War, headphones became a common accessory for record players. The technology flourished with the expansion of the American military industrial complex, and had been perfected just in time for the post-war consumer boom. For the first time, it was possible to limit the world of recorded sound to an audience of one, and without locking the door. Then came cassettes, and not long after, the Walkman. Now we the audience of one could go almost anywhere, shutting out the world with whatever cassettes (or, later, CDs) we brought with us.

Then came the mp3, and with it the portable mp3 player. The limit on the number of songs increased exponentially. The rise of smartphones and subscription streaming services shattered that limit too. Today, theoretically, we can "bring with us" every sound, every song, every concerto and opus, cakewalk and rag, frantic hardcore scream and Soundcloud rap, ever recorded.

It is enough to drive the imagination wild. Except

that as we gave our minds and curiosities free reign to traipse through this endless history, we did so increasingly as individuals. In fact, we were told that, outside of the individual, history had ended.

Probably just as well that we didn't notice that music as a *social phenomenon*, as something shared, debated, created and recreated on a mass scale, was slipping through our fingers. Considering the increasing isolation of urbanized life, we were better off retreating, wherever possible, into a bubble. If we can't eliminate the avatars of physical and psychic trauma that surround us in the modern city, if we see no route to a collective solution, if the collective solution cannot even occur to us, then better to keep these avatars of them at bay.

"The use of headphones," says Mark Fisher in his landmark book *Capitalist Realism*, "is significant here – pop is experienced not as something which could have impacts on public space, but as 'OedIpod' consumer bliss, a walling up against the social."[1]

Capital-rhythm

Capitalism has a rhythm, recognized in its productive capacities by Frederick Winslow Taylor and Henry Ford, noted and excoriated by Marx and EP Thompson. As objects became commodities, as the commodity became the dominant form of everything on the planet, and as commodity exchange their primary circulation, the gestures and tasks needed to construct them were timed, broken down, regimented and repeated ad infinitum. The rhythms of life came to be dominated not by the seasons, the rise and set of the sun, but by the hours, minutes and seconds it took to manufacture and sell. Our experience of time itself transformed radically.

[1] Mark Fisher, *Capitalist Realism: Is there No Alternative?* (Alresford: Zero Books, 2009) p.24.

Thompson, in 'Time, Work-Discipline, and Industrial Capitalism', argues as much, illustrating his point through the rise in ubiquity of the mechanical clock itself from the 1300s through to the early nineteenth century. Prior to the rise of the clock, time was kept not according to the ever-waning hour, minute or second, but according to the position of the sun in the sky, the melting of a winter's snow, the blossom of flowers on the tree. He cites multiple different measurements and pre-capitalist conceptions of time, from the Aran Islands to Algeria to Madagascar, as examples of the temporal and labor autonomy this afforded.[2]

The peasant farmer, small-time weaver, the shoemaker and blacksmith, ultimately owned their wares, only selling or giving away what they needed to survive or what was expected of them. What's more, to a small-but-significant degree, they could ponder in their toiling, mull over what did and didn't work in the fruits of their labor and what could be made better. They could experiment, apply intelligence and creativity to their craft. "Work-rhythms," as Thompson refers to them, could vary widely.

Most laborers and artisans didn't own a clock. But as the factory encroached on their lives, as their labor became the only thing they could sell, eventually, inevitably, the clock became essential. Even at home, in their retreat from drudgery, they couldn't afford to lose track of the hour. If they did, the doors might be locked on them when they arrived for their shift. A day's wages were lost. The progressive hegemony of "clock time" was instrumental in robbing laborers of control over what they

---

[2] E.P. Thompson, 'Time, Work-Discipline, and Industrial Capitalism', *Past & Present*, no. 38 (December 1967), https://www.sv.uio.no/sai/english/research/projects/anthropos-and-the-material/Intranet/economic-practices/reading-group/texts/thompson-time-work-discipline-and-industrial-capitalism.pdf.

produced, how much of it they produced, and for whom it might be produced.

It was part of a broader historical process by which the peasants and small artisans were uprooted from their common lands wholesale, their autonomy stripped. Locked in workshops (and they were frequently locked), their time belonged to someone else. The speed and efficiency of their movements were watched, increasingly demanding quotas placed on their productivity.

As "work-time" and "free-time" became distinct, free-time was now also under the sway of the clock. Capitalism's temporal patterns entrenched themselves everywhere they could. Here is Ellen Meiksins Wood in *Democracy Against Capitalism*:

> [I]f capitalism – with its juridically free working class and its impersonal economic powers – removes many spheres of personal and social activity from direct class control, human life generally is drawn more firmly than ever into the orbit of the production process. Directly or indirectly, the demands and discipline of capitalist production, imposed by the exigencies of capitalist appropriation, competition and accumulation, bring within their sphere of influence – and thus under the sway of capital – an enormous range of activity and exercise an unprecedented control over the organization of *time*, within and without the production process.[3]

All of life came to be dominated by the clock, each second an obligation to exchange value. At work, movements were broken down to their most basic, any

---
3 Ellen Meiksins Wood, *Democracy Against Capitalism: Renewing Historical Materialism* (London: Verso, 2016) p.61.

opportunity for curiosity eliminated. Tasks were mindless and repetitive, reduced to a dull, plodding rhythm for ten, twelve, sixteen hours a day. Time "off" was now when we did our best to ignore the fact that each passing second was returning us to the same mind-numbing monotony. If we were lucky we could stave off the reminders of time's passage through purchase of some item or experience that was itself created out of the same dead time. It's for this reason that the earliest labor disputes weren't about compensation for our time, but the *substance* of that time: how much of it we were expected to give, how much control over it we could exert.

The spread of clock-time was also a useful tool in capitalism's imperial spread. It was often met with resistance. Joe Zadeh, in 'The Tyranny of Time', cites the example among indigenous peoples of Australia during Britain's colonization:

> In Melbourne, churches and railway stations grew quickly on the horizon, bringing with them the hands, faces, bells and general cacophony of clock time. By 1861, a time ball was installed in the Williamstown lighthouse and Melbourne was officially synchronized to Greenwich Mean Time. British colonizers attempted to integrate indigenous peoples into their labor force with unsatisfactory results due to their unwillingness to sacrifice their own form of timekeeping. They did not believe in "meaningless toil" and "obedience to the clock," wrote the Australian sociologist Mike Donaldson. "To them, time was not a tyrant."[4]

The world's horizon expands, spatial barriers

---

[4] Joe Zadeh, 'The Tyranny of Time', *Noema Magazine* (3 June 2021), https://www.noemamag.com/the-tyranny-of-time.

are battered down. Distance is, paraphrasing Marx, annihilated by time. The technologies that, paraphrasing Marx, annihilate distance with time, also break down and over-mediate our experience, alienating us from each other and ourselves. The spectacle that captures our wonder cuts us off from our own agency. The world feels more beyond our control than ever. Situationist philosopher Guy Debord identified this paradox when he wrote in his 1967 *Society of the Spectacle* that "[t]his society eliminates geographical distance only to reap distance internally in the form of spectacular separation."[5]

In every corner of the globe, places that 500 years ago were the stuff of tall tales can now be touched, or at least learned about with relative accuracy. Except that most of us will never "see" them for ourselves. Rather, we will imagine ourselves in them through the film or photograph, the technologically reproducible image, the recorded sound. Cities grow outward and upward. It is people like us who perform the physical construction. Yet most of us will never know the skyscraper's top floor. History, now revealed as consummately changeable, either happens without us or to us, but never *because* of us. The rhythms of a commodified life blunt our individual and collective subjectivities, prevent us from fully living.

Capitalism's rhythm shapes our music...

This rise of commodity rhythm transformed not just how we listened to music – making it more widely available and attainable – but the form of the music itself. As capitalism spread across the planet, as rural life became increasingly urban, as nations were pillaged for the sake of primitive accumulation, cultural and artistic

---

[5] Guy Debord, *Society of the Spectacle* [1967], trans. by Donald Nicholson-Smith (New York: Zone Books, 1995) p.167, https://www.marxists.org/reference/archive/debord/society.htm.

expression dramatically changed.

What we understand as "popular music" ultimately exists because of this process. Before capitalism's rhythms embedded themselves in every facet of daily life, music's rhythmic structures could vary greatly. In some cases they tested the boundaries of what we presently take for granted as rhythm. In many instances, such as the *muezzin* in Asia Minor and the Maghreb, the rhythm, cadence and notes were built around the rhythm of the words. Northern European folk tale songs often took a similar approach. The beats of West African ceremonial dances evinced a rhythmic structure that was far deeper than the relatively one-dimensional rhythms of early American military marches.

It is well-known and much discussed by now that key elements of the blues – therefore American popular music and, to a certain extent, popular music the world over – can be traced back to the fieldwork songs of enslaved Africans and their descendants. Far less discussed is how intertwined this phenomenon was with the rise of capitalism and global empire. The rhythms and structures that began to take shape, morphing from old West African songs, also morphed around the need for constant and repetitive production, a pace that could keep up with a burgeoning global market for goods and commodities.

For the immediate descendants of those enslaved, the evolution of these sounds attempted to conceive a presence and future for themselves, what Clyde Woods, in *Development Arrested*, calls "blues epistemology." In the context of a Mississippi Delta and an American South reimposing tight control over Black labor and traditions, the blues was "channeling folk wisdom, descriptions of life and labor, travelogues, hoodoo, and critiques of individuals and institutions."[6]

The rise of popular music, music which came from the popular classes, necessitated the creation and consolidation of these same popular classes, bringing them all, in spite of whatever differences and variances they may have according to region or background, into a common world system. The need to standardize everything, to make everything commensurable, to make space, time, and human life a predictable formula, became an overarching imperative. Most often, it was a standardization violently imposed. But it also replaced provinciality with cosmopolitanism. And humans are rarely so easily predicted. Musicians both professional and itinerant were exposed to sonic conceptions from other parts of the globe they would have otherwise never experienced. Styles and traditions crossbred at rates they never had before, and all under the umbrella of a daily life unavoidably dominated by work, and increasingly anxious with its own regimentation. Virtually every song we know and love in the context of modernity is the result of this cosmopolitanizing process.

This is not to deny that the colonized world made essential contributions to the feel and sound of popular music; if anything the breadth of this contribution has yet to be fully acknowledged. Nor was this process one of sheer and absolute homogenization. Comparing the music of Fela Kuti with that of the Ramones yields stark contrasts, despite being made at virtually the same point in history. The particularities of Kuti's music reflect a specific point in the history of Nigeria characterized by a fast-paced spread of heavy industry during the 1970s oil boom through a society that had been historically heavily agricultural, the complex layering of different paces

---

[6] Clyde Woods, *Development Arrested: The Blues and Plantation Power in the Mississippi Delta* [1998] (London: Verso, 2017) p.43.

of life on top of each other, the quickening of traditional rhythms that had only recently lifted off the weight of colonial domination.

The Ramones, meanwhile, formed in a New York City that was coming apart at the seams. The post-war boom had bust, the city was bankrupt, whole neighborhoods were left to rot. In this context, aggressive simplicity, introduced and underlined by a near-mindless "1, 2, 3, 4," made sense. Same for their audience. Whatever their vast differences, they both reflected the basic reality that both Lagos, Nigeria, and New York City had been fully integrated into a global system of commodity production.

The common elements deployed in popular music are the subject of Mark Abel's *Groove: An Aesthetic of Measured Time*. Music, writes Abel, is inevitably an aestheticization of time. Our mental and emotional reaction to a note or beat is shaped by the note or beat that comes before, after, simultaneously. A song's resonance can only be achieved over the course of time, no matter how long or short, even if it is only the length of the song itself. Thus, the temporal mode of music under an entrenched capitalism reflects the experience of capitalist time.

Though there are vast differences between various genres and styles of popular music, virtually all assume a rhythmic pattern which Abel breaks down into four key elements: *metronomic time, syncopation, deep metricality,* and *back-beat*.

Metronomic time: the isochronous pulse, the regular and repetitive rhythm, the "1-2-3-4." Prior to the rise of industrial capitalism, it was not uncommon to hear forms of music whose pulse could vary greatly, even within the same composition. In some pre-modern genres – Gregorian plainchant for example, or the Muslim call to prayer known as the *muezzin* – rhythm was relatively unconstrained, free to bend and shift around the needs of the words being sung. Nineteenth century Romantic music often encouraged deviations from regular rhythm so that musical phrases could be fully articulated by performers. European classical music is well-known for shifts in tempo and use of different time signatures. In industrial capitalism, the rhythm of music learns to mimic the repetitive movements of the assembly line.

With a regular rhythm established – not unlike the sharp, steady rhythm of the assembly line or factory – the other sonic signatures of popular music serve to further tighten and intensify it.

Syncopation: the regular placement of other notes, beats or gestures between the beats of the "1-2-3-4," mostly on the half, quarter, or eighth, also as a pattern that is adhered to or deviated from to varying degrees. The vocals, the guitars, bass, keys, brass, the other percussive instruments; their own repetitions both fill the space between the beats and bring our awareness further into these spaces. Most importantly, these elements heighten a sense of anticipation, the knowledge that the movement just performed will be coming back around sooner or later, and most of the time sooner.

Deep metricality, or *multi-levelled meter* is difficult to describe, partly because it takes an approach to the very concept of meter and time signature that many music theorists will find up for debate. Suffice to say Abel is describing the phenomenon by which a single musical phrase of one instrument or singer may stretch well beyond the time it takes another to play theirs, and vice versa. A guitar part may have many more notes to hit in the same span of time that the bass hits theirs, interlocking with a percussion part that leaves space for the eighth or quarter notes to fill in the gaps between.

This leads to an experience of music in which instruments may appear to be playing different time signatures that nonetheless interlock. A "sonic hierarchy" is created in which certain sounds are accentuated and others serve to compliment. Melodies and harmonies find their own patterns to interweave with the rhythm. As the pattern builds out, so does it create divergence, at once further heightening anticipation and, conversely, anticipation for ways in which the pattern changes.

Finally, the *back-beat*: whereas previous musics with a regular rhythm may or may not have placed a particular emphasis on any number in the metronomic time, back-beat favors an "off" beat. Think of the military marches of John Phillip Souza, which place a balanced even emphasis on every beat from "1" to "4." By contrast, rock, blues and R&B almost always place emphasis on the "2" and "4." Listen for where the snare drum hits in any rock song or hip-hop sample, and it is obvious to pick out.[7]

Taken together, these four elements make for a distinct, tightly wound rhythmic experience. It is a sensibility based on anticipation and reward, in which the new is quickly integrated into the pre-existing. The world built for us by this arrangement of beats and notes becomes more complex, more subtle. It demands we open our attention to ever-greater depths but that we also inevitably return to a familiar pattern. At its most effective it creates a state in the listener at once hypnotic and deeply engaged.

Anyone who has spent any time in a workplace where the same products or services are repetitively produced can attest to the familiarity of this temporal structure. And not just in the traditional factories or

---

[7] The above is a very brief summary of the far more in-depth description provided in the book. Mark Abel, *Groove: An Aesthetic of Measured Time* (Leiden: Brill, 2014).

warehouses which in many parts of the world appear to be vanishing.

A barista in a coffee shop acclimates themselves to going between the cash register and the espresso machine, knowing that certain movements and gestures will always be part of the pattern, but knowing that there will inevitably be variations depending on the order. The product must be as standardized as possible so that it can be sold for a predictable price.

Phone jockeys in call centers memorize the beats of their script, but also prepare themselves for moments when they will need to improvise, even as some improvisations become more common than others, gaining their own predictability and being partially integrated into the script. In both cases, there is a regular rhythm of action to which the worker has learned to return. The popular song rewards a similar learned instinct.

Nor is this just happenstance, coincidence, or even something that we only unconsciously repeat. Berry Gordy, record producer and founder of Motown Records, frequently claimed the chugging rhythmic signature of his label's legendary soul sound came to him through years of working on the assembly line of Detroit's once-iconic auto plants.

With this rhythmic structure dominant, it seems fitting that it also reach into influencing a song's tone and thematic content. Tony Iommi, perhaps the most influential guitarist in the history of heavy metal, teaches us something similar. The future guitarist of Black Sabbath famously lost the tips of two of his fingers on his last day working as a welder in a sheet metal plant in Birmingham, England. Ozzy Osbourne remembers being traumatized by the industrial killing he performed in one of the city's slaughterhouses. The influence of this deafening repetition and industrialized violence is evident in Black

Sabbath's first three albums. "Literally, this was heavy metal in life influencing heavy metal in sound," wrote Bryan Reesman.[8]

The linkage between industrial production and the sonic structure of modern popular music is clear. What of this linkage though? How does the dominance of this temporal structure bode for us; we with no control over how we work or what is done with that work?

In an essay written with George Simpson, 'On Popular Music', Theodor Adorno heard the reproduction of industrial rhythm as proof that popular music was a deceitful fetter on the imagination.[9] To him, the apparent freedom of popular music was a mirage. Its standardized rhythms content us with the rigid patterns of a commodified life, almost as a kind of hypnosis, lulling us just enough to make the idea of going back into work bearable, a bigger cage masquerading as liberation. This colonization of our consciousness is yet another safeguard against the overthrow of a fundamentally unjust system. Popular music, therefore, is in fundamental agreement with countless other cultural mechanisms designed to put control over our own lives just beyond reach.

...and the rhythm of our cities

Return to the city, filled as it is with reminders that our lives can never be fullfilling. These are so numerous, so quotidian, that we barely notice them anymore. Hostile architecture – from rounded bus benches to shiny metal spikes poking out from flat surfaces – delineates

---

[8] Bryan Reesman, 'How Birmingham Shaped Black Sabbath and Heavy Metal', *Discogs.com* (9 October 2020), https://blog.discogs.com/en/black-sabbath-birmingham-connection-heavy-metal/.

[9] Theodor W. Adorno, 'On Popular Music', in *Cultural Theory and Popular Culture: A Reader*, ed. by John Storey (Athens, GA: The University of Georgia Press, 1998).

the limits on a place's possibility. We cannot "use" them for anything other than a quick glance as we pass them by, or at the very most a short wait, sitting, but never lying down, and repurposing only by crossing the arbitrary lines of legality.

Recent decades have given rise to the phenomenon urbanists describe as "pseudo-public space." Contemporary parks are increasingly policed to ensure they are populated by "the right kind of people." Observe the unhoused person being hassled along by the cops or sanitation services. Or the way in which those deemed undesirable, be they unpermitted protesters or unruly youth, are targeted in these places ostensibly open to public gathering.

Then there are the places we simply can't go. Which, if we really think about it, make up the vast majority of any given city. High-rise buildings have increased the amount of occupied space in the urban landscape. And yet, if any of us attempted to walk through their front doors without the right permission or at the wrong time of day, we would be ordered to go elsewhere or charged with trespassing. Forget any challenge to how these spaces might be used; even basic movement within them is denied. These characteristics, on top of rising housing costs, decline in wages, cuts to public services and a host of other attacks, reveal a great deal about exactly whom the city is built for.

Enter Henri Lefebvre, the French Marxist sociologist. For him, the biggest danger was already hiding in plain sight: the wholesale subjugation of daily life by the logic of capital; a regimentation so airtight that even the very idea of an alternative becomes nonsense; the elimination of genuine chance, spontaneous creativity, and authentic adventure. He could already see this specter's head looming with the rise of consumer culture and the globalized world order in the wake of the Second World War.

In *The Production of Space*, he examined how this phenomenon manifested itself in the post-war city. For Lefebvre, all space – rural and urban – was in danger of becoming entirely abstract. This "abstract space," while apparently homogenous, actually encompassed a wide variety of architectural, aesthetic, political and juridical tools working in tandem. In Lefebvre's words:

> They are different ways of achieving the same outcome: the reduction of the 'real,' on one hand, to a 'plan' existing in a void and endowed with no other qualities, and, on the other hand, to the flatness of a mirror, of an image, of pure spectacle under an absolutely cold gaze.[10]

In other words, abstract space is easy, predictable, and appositely inhuman. It reflects back the ease with which it can be used to dominate and keep order. Complications, including those introduced by pesky autonomous humans, are absent.

For those select few who can afford it, life looks a lot like Hudson Yards in New York. This is a gleaming fortress of luxury apartments, trendy shops and restaurants built on a massive platform hovering over the busy West Side rail yards. As denoted by the name and shape of the hideous architectural structure the Vessel, situated inside the courtyard, residents of Hudson Yards can cocoon themselves away from the chaotic ebbs and flows of New York City, picking and choosing when they might enter into them, shielded from the comings and goings of capital that are literally a constant beneath their feet.

For the rest of us are far more subject to those same

---

10 Henri Lefebvre, *The Production of Space* [1974], trans. by Donald Nicholson-Smith (Oxford: Blackwell, 1991) p.287.

ebbs and flows. The modern city is designed not for us to inhabit so much as to be ushered through, so that we might be at an intended place at an intended time, to work, to socialize or rest appropriately (and lately for dwindling lengths of time), and to otherwise refrain from disturbing the flows of capital.

The authoritarian domination of space can never be absolute, though corporations and city governments will try. Nonetheless, Lefebvre also concluded that even with various needs and desires competing for influence, cities have rhythms. Function and design of the city promote or discourage certain kinds of movement or uses at any given time, depending on the needs of who ultimately controls it. Thus the needs of commodity production, time-sensitive and tightly wound, translate into the rhythms of different forms of space. Be they office buildings or public parks, fish markets or train terminals, commercial areas, schools, residential neighborhoods, or construction sites, there is a rhythm to be analyzed – a "rhythmanalysis" as Lefebvre coined it: predictable times when spaces are occupied or not, and in what way.

Today, no rhythm dominates the city more than the algorithm. The latter, of course, is mostly thought in relation to the web-centric programs that have become essential to our daily lives – particularly as a social life that might constitute the "real" in Lefebvre's view is increasingly replaced by social media. The algorithm relies on its own rhythm, its own sequence of events that metabolizes chance with ease. The linguistic overlap between these two words, rhythm and algorithm, is not coincidence.

The flows of capital and commodity, and therefore our livelihoods, are dependent on the algorithm. It tracks the delivery driver traversing the city's streets to make sure food prepared in a restaurant reaches its consumer by a set time. It monitors bathroom breaks and other "idle time" for fulfillment center workers. It organizes data of our habits and behaviors at work, at home, even on the streets, into usable parcels that cajole us to buy or sell, to reward us or punish us. As the algorithm grows, as its content becomes more complex, it becomes less about predicting our behavior than subtly shaping it, tightening the pace of our movements and lives.

Lefebvre had a word to describe this fevered state in the city. He called it "arrhythmia," not unlike how a doctor describes the heartbeat of a sick patient. Our cities are sick because their inhabitants are sick, coercively saddled with an anxiety that never fully abates. The possibility of the city, this massive concatenation of potential and human imagination, is cut off from us, our individual and collective subjectivity deflected at every meaningful turn.

In *Rebel Cities*, David Harvey deftly sketches this gap and how the dilemma mirrors that of human society more generally:

> The right to the city is, therefore, far more than a right of individual or group access to the resources that the city embodies: it is a right to change and reinvent the city more after our hearts' desire. It is, moreover, a collective rather than an individual right, since reinventing the city inevitably depends upon the exercise of a collective power over the processes of urbanization. The freedom to make and remake ourselves and our cities is, I want to argue, one of the most precious yet most neglected of our human rights.[11]

Inspired by Lefebvre, Harvey deliberately mentions the right to "change ourselves" in the same dialectical breath as "changing the city," illustrating how the

---
11 David Harvey, *Rebel Cities* (London: Verso, 2019) p.4.

present cleavage between the two robs both. As the urban environment is increasingly alienated from us, so do we become more alienated from ourselves.

Music (and capital) remaking space

With this in mind, we should consider how capital's spatial arrangements and its many musical modes supplement each other. Both music and space have rhythms. How, therefore, does music interact with space, if at all? More to the point, *in whose interest* does this interaction take place?

A story that illustrates this comes from the failed 1917 experiment of the great early modernist composer Erik Satie. His *musique d'ameublement,* or "furnishing music," was a series of short compositions intended to be played while a room's inhabitants went about other business, as if to make the space more pleasant to be in and amenable to other activities. At the time, it was unusual, if not entirely unheard of, for live music to be incidental to space rather than its focal point.

The experiment, alas, was unsuccessful. Satie could not overcome his fame and notoriety. People attended not to chat and move about as his music played in the background, but to hear his music. Satie was outraged. The story goes that during the performances he would lambaste attendees. "For Heaven's sake!" he shouted at them. "Move around! Don't listen!" His patrons were understandably bewildered. This, after all, was a composer whose musical performances had outraged and scandalized the bourgeoisie so many times before.

One hundred years later, the use of music to create "ambience," to instill a certain mood into a space – whether those within it are paying attention or not – is commonplace. Composers from John Cage to Brian Eno have taken up Satie's mantle. If music cannot "change the world" in a literal sense, it seems that it can nonetheless change our experience of the space around us. Sound can be used in a space to match our moods, to streamline our intentions. The sudden popularity on YouTube and Spotify of "Lofi Study Beats" exemplifies how ever-present this has become.

Though these specific forms are more recent, the use of music to maintain dominance and compliance is not. Six years after Satie admonished his patrons for not sufficiently ignoring his music, Major General George Owen Squier of the United States Army founded the company Wired, Inc., which developed the technology to transmit music into subscribing businesses, office buildings, and other workplaces. Before his death in 1934, Squier renamed the company "Muzak."

Muzak didn't own any music rights, so to keep costs down, it produced its own, hiring bands and composers to record originals. The music was mildly pleasant and inoffensive. "Basically, jazz and big band music with all the edges sanded off," as Joe Veix describes it.[12] According to company executives, the songs were designed to be ignored, a pleasing undercurrent working on the subconscious of listeners rather than grabbing their attention.

The intent, according to Muzak, was to make spaces of commerce more welcoming, both easing consumers into easily parting with their money and boosting productivity in employees. Studies were produced claiming that workers' efficiency increased anywhere from 9 to 38 percent. Though the veracity of these studies was questionable, the company was a success. As it grew and evolved it employed more research and scientific

---

12 Joe Veix, 'Fitter, Happier, More Productive: The Odd History of 'Productivity Music'', *Work in Progress blog* (17 January 2019).

technique to move the mood of its listeners. By the 1950s, Muzak had its own in-house orchestra, and unveiled a method called "Stimulus Progression," alternating fifteen minutes of music with fifteen minutes of silence. Once again, company-funded studies had shown that these intervals mitigated "listener fatigue," in turn increasing productivity and overall feelings of ease.

Muzak is no longer the juggernaut of background it once was, even if its name is now synonymous with the syrupy and anodyne. The company filed for bankruptcy in 2009 before being bought out by its competitor Mood Music, which itself went belly-up in 2013. But corporations are, to this day, still interested in shaping our moods with music. In 2011, brand consulting firm Heartbeats International – who can count Coca-Cola, Breitling, and Waldorf Hotels among its list of clients – produced a pamphlet titled 'Uncovering a Musical Myth: A Survey on Music's Impact in Public Spaces.'

"Just as interior design is part of the in-store experience," the pamphlet starts, "music has become an important competitive tool for business owners." It goes on to claim, as Muzak did, that workers' productivity increases with music played during work hours. Relying on surveys of different age groups, it asserts that 46 percent of those surveyed find that music makes the work environment "more relaxed." The number increases to 56 percent with 16-to-24-year-olds. "The survey results clearly show that music is a good investment. It creates a better atmosphere, makes employees feel better, and helps them work more productively."[13]

During the coronavirus pandemic, the same ideas

---

[13] 'Uncovering a Musical Myth: A Survey On Music's Impact in Public Spaces', *Heartbeats International* (2011), http://www.soundslikebranding.com/myth/Uncovering_a_musical_myth.pdf.

found their way into a new workplace: the home. An April 2020 article in the *Guardian* provided a "how-to" guide for boosting work-from-home productivity through music. This time relying not on pseudo-scientific study but on pop psychology, the piece urges its readers to

> Kick off the day with a trick from music therapy. The concept is known as the iso principle, which is a technique therapists use to alter the mood of a patient. The therapist will match music to how the patient is feeling, and then gradually alter the songs to achieve the desired mood state.[14]

And thus, by the end of the day, the listener-worker will have reached a high productivity level, coupled with a greater feeling of ease and accomplishment. The question, however, remains. In whose interest? For whose benefit? Who reaps the greatest from these spikes in productivity, from our attempts to trick ourselves into believing we aren't really at work as we work?

We need only consider the decades of wage stagnation, and its accompanying, never-ending rise in corporate profits, to answer this. Even if music's impact on the listener-worker is entirely "in their head," if it merely makes them *feel* as if they are more relaxed and productive on the job, in the view of the employer, it has done its job. If music under capitalism can impose the logic of exploitation on our leisure time, then music in the workplace appears to blur the line in the opposite direction. Listen closely. Adorno is chuckling bitterly in his grave.

---

14 Cass Balzer, 'Music can boost your productivity while working from home – here's how', *Guardian* (15 April 2020), https://www.theguardian.com/us-news/2020/apr/15/music-productivity-working-from-home.

SONGS IN AN ALIEN CITY

Geographies of control and sounds of a deflected future

The authoritarian city has also learned these lessons. Music and sound are used to keep its rhythms working – where we can be, when we can be there, and in what capacity. Complimenting hostile architecture, we have classical music blasted into London train stations late at night, designed to keep the riffraff out. Heavy-handed policing finds use for Long Range Acoustic Devices in dispersing protesters. And no pseudo-public space is quite complete without the heavy regulation or outright prohibition of busking. In all, the assertion is the same: *this is not your space… you may not use or reinvent it as you see fit… you are here only insofar as you are allowed to be here…*

But if music can be used to influence behaviors and outlooks, there is no more successful advent than that of the ubiquitous streaming service. None more ubiquitous than Spotify. At first blush, it seems a fair trade-off: if the city is not ours to explore, to remake in our own image, then at least we can discover and explore the world of music as we travel through it.

As research in recent years has shown, the scope of this exploration can also be extremely limited. Hence the algorithm, which always has a suggestion for what you would "like" to hear next. The jarring sensation of hearing something in stylistic contrast to what you just heard, a potential invitation to notice what is around you, is mitigated. We travel through the space half-awake, lulled to the degree required for us to never disrupt its flow.

Occasionally we may peer at our phones to see who this "new" artist is. Perhaps we tuck their name in the back of our mind to look up later. Do we always remember? And if the artist sounds so similar to the one that came before, will it matter if we forget?

If we rely on streaming services for any deep biographical information, we'll be disappointed. Most don't provide much in the way of notes, the individual musicians who played on a track, the engineers who helped find a sound, the circumstances in which it was found. The tactility of discovering new music – crate-diving for old records or flipping through CDs in the record store, of having our curiosity piqued into an artist's life and lived experience, the time and place in which they recorded – is diminished in this new mode of listening. It is the necessary musical component of a world in which social life – what Lefebvre might have called "the real" – is replaced by a social media increasingly unafraid to flaunt its own financialization.

This dehistoricization is present on the other end of the spectrum, in what the artists themselves are softly coerced into writing and recording. Landing a spot on one of Spotify's coveted official playlists can be a boon for the artist, leading to more plays and more fans, perhaps more buyers. And with the biggest streamers doling out a measly half-cent per play, who can blame them for chasing this goal? The siphoning of music toward more "marketable" sounds, which many in the music industry feared would be completely smashed with the arrival of online streaming, finds a new and insidious method of reproduction. According to musician and writer Ted Mair:

> When songs are uploaded to Spotify they can be "pitched" to the platform, in the hope that they would make it onto playlists. This is an artist's main hope for exposure. In order to make these playlists a song needs to capture the imagination of those at Spotify who curate their playlists within its opening seconds. Because of this, many have noted trends emerging of shorter songs which encapsulate their choruses within around ten seconds. For

example, Lil Pump's "Gucci Gang", released in 2017, clocks in at 2:04. The chorus of the song hits by 16 seconds, preceded by an intro which teases the hook. This a condensed form of music which is built to gain exposure through streaming services.[15]

Certain sounds are promoted, others are relegated to the margins. And though we can always skip a track, the algorithm inexorably pulls us in its direction. Attention-spans diminish, desires are deflected and neutralized just as quickly as they are created, and with them our imagination is corralled. Much like how redeveloped neighborhoods and town centers erase the history of a place, denying us the possibility of discovering difference beneath the anodyne, so does the algorithm-curated playlist encourage a "gentrification of music," a narrowing of possibility.

This accounts for what Mark Fisher called "the slow cancellation of the future." We are well-acquainted with this structure of feeling, even if we do not have the language to pinpoint it. The feeling that nothing is new, that something in time's passage, something in *time itself*, has short-circuited, leaving us unmoored and frantically grasping. According to Fisher, this atemporality is particularly present in popular music:

> Consider the fate of the concept of 'futuristic' music. The 'futuristic' in music has long ceased to refer to any future that we expect to be different; it has become an established style, much like a particular typographical font. Invited to think of the futuristic, we still come up with

15 Ted Mair, 'New Hegemonies: Streaming Platforms and Music Production', *Verso blog* (26 February 2021), https://www.versobooks.com/blogs/5006-new-hegemonies-streaming-platforms-and-music-production.

something like the music of Kraftwerk, even though this is now as antique as Glenn Miller's big band jazz was when the German group began experimenting with synthesizers in the early 1970s.[16]

Fisher connects this to the social changes that have unmoored us in the material sense. The casualization of labor, attacks on social services, cuts in budgets for public schools and the arts, the unfettered rise in housing costs, the crushing of unions and social movements that have historically provided working people a sense of shared destiny, the same processes that have transformed the city into an alien landscape; all have contributed to a crisis in social cohesion. Margaret Thatcher's old dictum, "there is no such thing as society" lives on. In society's place is the lonely crowd, the collection of anxious and precarious shuffling through space. The world around us and its potential future, are beyond our control, immutable as far as we are concerned. Attempting to (re-)create them is a fool's errand.

Just as the city flows along the rhythms of commodity, the streaming playlist, personalized to our temperaments, delivered into our ear, allows for that overarching rhythm to continue uninterrupted. With the border between work and leisure increasingly dissolving, these rhythms find their way into the home.

Capital, having fully entrenched itself in virtually every corner of the planet, now turns inward. It looks for new and novel ways to dispossess us. Our intended escape from the pain and heartache around us ensures their survival at our expense. Contentment with – or at the very least resignation to – our exploitation and atomization goes full-spectrum. Music becomes a

[16] Mark Fisher, *Ghosts of My Life: Writings on Depression, Hauntology and Lost Futures* (Arlesford: Zero Books, 2014) p.9.

supplement to spatial control, buttressing what Fredric Jameson calls in his description of late capitalist architecture (and in a clever inversion of Marx) "the domination of space over time."[17]

An immutable and ever-present present lords over us. Dismal? Absolutely. But it is not the whole story. Like every towering and apparently impregnable edifice, it has its cracks. It's within then that we find the point of departure, the point where a new dialectic of time and space, of musical rebellion, is constructed.

---

17 Fredric Jameson, 'Postmodernism, Or, The Cultural Logic of Late Capitalism', *New Left Review,* no. 146 (July/August 1984) pp.59-92.

Part Two
Survival Rhythms

"People bury the parts of history they don't like,
pave it over like African cemeteries beneath Manhattan
skyscrapers."
Alyssa Cole, *When No One Is Watching*

"They said it's not enough
Just to shoot us down
It's a sound that's systematized
Yeah, it's a noise just to drown us out"
Algiers, 'Irony. Utility. Pretext.'

Music as a threat

On November 23rd, 2012, Jordan Davis, a seventeen-year-old African-American teenager, was shot and killed in the parking lot of a gas station in Jacksonville, Florida. The man who shot him, Michael Dunn, had parked his car near the SUV where Davis and his friends were sitting. On the SUV's stereo played the song 'Beef' by Lil Reese, featuring Lil Durk and Fredo Santana. Dunn, a white, 45-year-old software developer, reportedly complained to his fiancé, who was in the passenger seat, about "that rap crap," though she would later claim he called it "thug music." After an argument over the volume of the music, Dunn returned to his car, took a handgun out of the glove box, and pumped ten rounds into the SUV. Davis died of his injuries.

Jordan Davis was not killed because of "loud music." He was killed because Dunn was (and is) a self-entitled racist. Dunn was willing to resort to violence to maintain the dominance over public space he, as a white man, felt he was owed. Parallels were drawn to the murder of Trayvon Martin – which took place in Florida mere months before. The state's retrograde "Stand Your Ground" laws, that allow for the use of deadly force if a civilian "feels threatened," came under fire. Critics rightly argued that the law gave carte blanche for racists to resort to violence.

The role that the music played was secondary, but nonetheless prescient. Dunn resided in Satellite Beach, a small coastal city two hours south of Jacksonville. Its population is ninety-five percent white, its average household income almost twice the national average. One is particularly susceptible in such environments to racist rhetoric about the dangers of the "urban jungle." Some part of Dunn's psyche – a large part in fact – heard these fictionalized dangers spouted back to him in the beats blasting from an SUV. Dunn admitted as much in a blog post published during his trial:

> I would offer that, rather than rail against the 'Stand Your Ground' laws, people take a look at the violence and lifestyle that the "Gangsta Rap" music and the "thug life" promote. The jails are chock full of young black men – and so are the cemeteries. Gun laws have nothing to do with it. The violent sub-cultures that so many young men become enthralled with are

destroying an entire generation.¹

The notion that Dunn understood anything about rap or hip-hop is *prima facie* ridiculous. Which is probably why his argument didn't work. In 2014, after two trials, he was convicted of first-degree murder and sentenced to life in prison without the possibility of parole.

Less than two years later, on July 5th, 2016, two police officers approached 37-year-old Alton Sterling outside of a Triple S Food Mart in Baton Rouge, Louisiana. The officers later claimed that they were responding to a call from the convenience store clerk about someone causing a disturbance in the parking lot. Speaking to media, the clerk was clear that Sterling had not been the person he called about.

On the contrary, Sterling was known and liked in the area. Those who interacted with him called him "CD Man." The night police shot and killed him, he was working the makeshift stall he always worked, selling bootleg CDs to passersby.

Sterling's reliance on informal and semi-legal cultural economies was partly due to the explosion in what sociologist Loïc Wacquant calls "hyperincarceration" of surplus populations in the United States and the racial disproportionalities therein. Baton Rouge's population is more than fifty percent Black. Its poverty rate is over 26 percent, twice the national average. Like many other Black men in the United States – long home to the largest prison population in the world – Alton Sterling had done time. After his release, his criminal record prevented him from finding gainful legitimate employment. But this says more

---

1 This quotation is from a now-dead blog originally written by Dunn, retrieved in Alexander Billet, 'On White Thugs Like Michael Dunn and the Scapegoating of Hip-Hop', *Red Wedge*, 15 February 2014, http://www.redwedgemagazine.com/atonal-notes/on-white-thugs-like-michaeldunn-and-the-scapegoating-of-hip-hop.

about how the carceral state continues to design our lives – particularly the lives of the poor – than it does about either Sterling or the community he served. Selling bootleg CDs was one among a limited array of options to make ends meet. Sterling remembered regular customers and their musical tastes. If he did not have an album that someone was looking for, he would make double-sure to have it next time they came by.

The day after his death, friends, customers and other community members held a vigil in front of the Triple S. The white foldable table he used to display CDs still sat from the night before in front of the store. By the end of the night, it was covered in messages to Sterling written in marker. In the following days, protests against the Baton Rouge Police Department swelled in size. Over a hundred were arrested. In March of 2018, after what it claimed was a thorough investigation, the Louisiana attorney general announced it would not be bringing charges against the two cops who shot and killed Sterling.

The murders of Alton Sterling and Jordan Davis point to a deeper logic when it comes to confronting spatial arrhythmia in the context of racial capitalism. Both murders highlight the interplay of three factors. First, the way in which oppressed and/or exploited populations are discouraged or prohibited from occupying certain spaces at all. Second, the way in which specific ways of occupying space culturally – including music – are viewed as a threat to those spaces. And third, the resultant potential of these musical and cultural expressions to disrupt the rhythm and flow of authoritarian urban space.

Arrhythmia and anachronism

To exist in authoritarian space is to dwell amidst confounding disparity. Wealthy regions abutting underdeveloped ones – not despite but *because* of each other. Skyscrapers on top of slums. Gated communities a stone's throw from ghettoes. Streets of trendy shops and brand-new condos, the occupants of run-down tenements around the corner made increasingly invisible before they are uprooted entirely.

All of this indicates, quite bluntly, that segregation is real, present, and persistent. In an American context, the very word "segregation" suggests a structure of separation purely racial in its content – one that mainstream history books tell us ended in the wake of the Civil Rights movement. The narrative goes similarly in other countries with a history of institutional and geographic racism (which is to say all of them). Segregation, apartheid; all, we are assured, are in civilization's rearview mirror.

As a spatial relationship, however, segregation is far from a thing of the past. For every school desegregated, every racist housing covenant struck down, every affirmative action program or reparation, there's the neglect of affordable housing to contend with, the underfunding of already poor public schools, the cramming of more and more bodies into the most systematically deprived areas.

Segregation, *de facto* in place of *de jure*, has become more entrenched alongside the proliferation of "urban renewal" projects, folded into the rhythms of gentrification and progress. It wouldn't be an exaggeration to say that the push to renewal is only possible if it includes the pushing out of undesirables, the eviction of poor people (disproportionately of color), the fracturing and scattering of working-class neighborhoods.

In this context, spaces in which these people can autonomously see and recreate themselves become rare. Free and affordable recreation dwindles as libraries, community centers and independent arts spaces shutter. And work, even well-paying work, is a space where none of us can truly and freely decide where to put our creative attention.

All of this is an inextricable part of Lefebvre's urban arrhythmia. If the drive to squeeze every bit of labor and profit out of public space is a constant one, then it has not – and by its nature cannot – solve the human problem. Commodification so often undermines its own aspirations regarding efficiency.

Yes, workers ostensibly may be ushered to work quicker if there are fewer places to linger and relax. But a lack of affordable housing pushes workers further and further from their place of employment. Attacks on public transport – from budget and service cuts to privatization – don't help matters either. And this doesn't begin to address what the commodified city plans to do with those who can't find employment.

A truly democratic city would be more supple, able to respond with equanimity to the needs and movements of its people. The only response the authoritarian city has in its toolkit is punishment. Legal or economic, the result is the same: an ever-tightening restriction on where and when the poor, the surplus, the racialized, are allowed to exist.

As space's status as commodity morphs and doubles in on itself, as its rhythms and movements become more erratic, so does the need to police it also increase. Thus, the bloated police budgets, the hostile architecture, the blasting of classical music in train stations, the cops' training to be on the lookout for troublemakers and undesirables (categories that are both, almost always, racialized).

This is the nature of segregation. It is never simply spatially enforced; it is lived temporally. The lives and experiences people are segregated *into* is one of material lack. In a sense it is one in which certain people are forcibly "left behind," enduring a process in which they are denied all the resources a moment in history theoretically has to offer.

We are not at any loss for examples. Think of Skid Row: a tent city existing on the sidewalks of barely half a square mile in downtown Los Angeles. The area contains an estimated 8,000 unhoused residents, around 85 percent of them Black or Hispanic. In the 1970s and 80s, city officials openly referred to Skid Row as a "containment zone." Laws against sleeping on the street were vigorously enforced elsewhere, in practice forcing them into an area where tourism was unlikely. More recent decades have seen a return of these kinds of ordinances.[2]

Or consider Grenfell Tower in London. True, the large-scale postwar construction of affordable housing estates across Britain means that, even today, you can still find these estates in relatively prosperous areas. Grenfell was in the Borough of Kensington and Chelsea, one of the richest in London. Even here – or perhaps especially here – the lower income, disproportionately non-white residents of Grenfell were expected to squeeze tighter and tighter together until they disappeared altogether. The cheapest building materials were used to update the building, safety equipment was not up to code, and residents' concerns were ignored for years. The resulting fire killed more than seventy people in June 2017.

There are plenty of words that can be used to describe this kind of social organization: unjust, criminal, unforgivable travesty. "Social murder" is what the left-wing then-shadow chancellor John McDonnell called it. When considering the interaction of space and time, however, a particularly useful concept is that of *anachronism*. More specifically, we might say that those of us who are

---

[2] Daniel Flaming and Gary Blasi, 'Los Angeles: Why tens of thousands of people sleep rough', *BBC* (19 September 2019).

subject to such systematic deprivations and indignities, forced to scrape and struggle to catch up on societies' peripheries are "anachronized." These are lives lived literally out of step with the rhythms of contemporary modernity. Every structure and institution shaped after the needs of capital – from the lack of fulfilling work to the "no loitering" sign – ensures this.

Sixty years ago, the situationists, in their endeavors to find new uses for public space, came up against this. In 'Salvaging Situationism: Race and Space', Andrea Gibbons recounts the 1958 attempt of Abdelhafid Khatib, an Algerian member of the Situationist International, to map and analyze the flow of Paris' streets.

This was among the first of what should have been many "psychogeographical surveys," practical poetic experiments that sought to interrogate the way urban space was increasingly designed to alienate and disempower, all with the aim of radically reimagining the city as a site of liberation.[3]

The problem that Khatib and his co-conspirators encountered was that Paris had imposed a curfew, and it was specifically directed at Arabs. Algerians were fighting for independence from French colonial rule. Algerians in France were protesting in support. The racist curfew was an attempt to crack down on these protests. Khatib was arrested twice while on *dérive*, each time spending the night in jail.[4] To French police, the notion of an Arab man moving freely through the city – let alone contemplating and reimagining it – was, once again, a threat.

We don't need to think very hard to find contemporary parallels to this. Cops, managers, and entitled

[3] Andrea Gibbbons, 'Salvaging Race and Space', *Salvage* (November 2015).
[4] The situationist meaning of the term *dérive* was that of "urban drift," of letting chance and instinct guide one through the space rather than that of accepted rules of its designers or rulers.

neo-yuppies are all too eager to tell people of color how they can use a park, that they are being too loud in the museum, or question their right to sit in a coffee shop. The domination of space over time, like most of everything else under capitalism, remains extremely racialized. It is worth juxtaposing this with Khatib's experience because it recenters the impulse to recreate, to remake the urban environment into one more suited to the needs of those who have been denied its full scope and potential. It also illustrates that there can be no psychogeography, no inquiry into a space's history or its interaction with our psychological states, without confronting histories and presents of racism and segregation. It's through this lens that we can better interrogate the rhythmic realities of the city.

As it is now, this possibility of exploration is so stymied as to be almost exclusively limited to the domestic sphere. As Cynthia Cruz writes in *The Melancholia of Class*:

> When all that remains of the cities are glass-encased shopping malls, corporate banks, and chain drugstores, there is no place left to retreat except inside one's living space – if, of course, one is fortunate enough to have one. These spaces are sites of survival for the working class because they allow for pockets of time where one can escape from the endless onslaught of work and worries connected to a life of precarity.[5]

There are wrinkles in this insight. The first is what we have already grasped, the way in which histories of racism and colonialism can amplify modes of isolation. It is also worth noting that, for a great many working-class people, the stressors of the outside world can transform

---

5 Cynthia Cruz, *The Melancholia of Class: A Manifesto for the Working Class* (London: Repeater, 2021) p.180.

their homes from safe havens into sites of hellish abuse.

Nonetheless, the observation is prescient. A life on the margins can make the home the only space working and oppressed people have open to them for the purpose of survival and creativity. This does not necessarily mean that the possibility of creative resistance is blunted. In some respects, it becomes more explosive.

Jean-Paul Sartre, in his 1940 book *The Imaginary*, attempts to sketch the relationship between human imagination and existence. A precursor to his definitive *Being and Nothingness*, Sartre posits human consciousness as ultimately intentional, setting himself up to argue that a life lived by the imposed rules of social class, race, gender, and so on, is essentially a life lived in bad faith. This is not to blame those who are trapped in such an existence; ideology and the realities of poverty are insidious things. It is to say that there is an imperative in human consciousness for freedom. Even in its most weakened state, it impels us forward.

Thus the imagination. In *The Imaginary*, Sartre argues that we rely on it in intrinsic ways. To imagine an object is to posit it as "irreal," imbued with qualities we ascribe to it based on past knowledge and our attitude toward that object. When we perceive a chair in front of us, we can only see one side at a time. That it is standing upright prompts us to picture the angles of it we can't see. We create an image that fills the gap of perception.

Navigating the world requires a synthesis of lived experience, knowledge, and any number of resulting images of what might be. To experience the real, we must employ the unreal. It is a process willingly employed by all artists, including musicians and composers. It necessarily relies on the imperfections and improvisations of the artists themselves. An original composition is made up more of the gaps than the certainties, letting unknowns and experiments carry the creator's instinct and inspiration.

Imagine, then, the working-class composer. Increasingly isolated into smaller and smaller spaces, the interstitials of urban life, surrounded by environments repeating the mantras of "no trespassing." They see and hear the world as it is, and contrast it with how they would like it. It is here, with the aid of whatever instrument or recording program they can access, that the musical process takes flight.

Unruly notes

Pull back the focus: from the street corner to the international border. The drive of profit and accumulation has always necessitated the deliberate underdevelopment of regions, countries, even entire continents, be it European colonialism's subjugation of Africa[6] and Latin America[7], or capitalism's systematic deprivation of resources to Black America.[8] These drives push people together and apart, sometimes half a planet away. The globalized economy – which, contrary to rumors of its demise, is strong as ever, albeit with more nationalistic inflections – ensures that the margins of every region will, eventually, inevitably, collide and comingle.

The frustrating and wonderful cultural contradiction produced by this is that every music genre is at once highly specific to its time and place and utterly indifferent to them. It is impossible to imagine the sound and

---

6 See Walter Rodney, *How Europe Underdeveloped Africa* (London: Bogle-L'Ouverture Publications, 1972).

7 See Eduardo Galleano, *Open Veins of Latin America: Five Centuries of the Pillage of a Continent* [1973], trans. by Cedric Belfrage (New York: Monthly Review Press, 1997).

8 See Manning Marable, *How Capitalism Underdeveloped Black America: Problems in Race, Political Economy, and Society* [1983] (Boston: South End Press, 2015).

rhythm of reggae originating in Rome, Italy in the 1940s; no, this is a sound intimately entangled with the political turmoil that followed the end of colonialism in Jamaica in the 1960s and 70s. The songs of that time and place *sound like* they emerged from that time and place.

Yet even this intensely specific genre was the result of cross-acculturation. Precursor forms of ska and rocksteady were heavily influenced by American jazz and R&B records as well as Caribbean calypso and mento. What reggae brought, among other elements, was a slower and more intense beat taken from Rastafari Nyabinghi drumming. In some ways, reggae is as much a music of the Black Atlantic as it is of Jamaica, a hybrid of different genres and sounds that themselves emerged from diasporas of dispossession and slavery, converging on a specific place and time to become more than the sum of its parts.

It's this same phenomenon that gave rise to almost every popular genre of modern music, from jazz and blues to rock and roll and disco, hip-hop and punk to Afrobeat and K-pop. The late communist and jazz musician Fred Ho calls this process "kreolization."[9] He describes it as "the free and voluntary intermingling, cultural synthesis and crossfertilization which occurs at the bottom of society, among the varying oppressed peoples."[10] Ho then takes this a step further, arguing that kreolization is a process "intrinsically related to resistance to oppression in a socio-political context."[11]

---

9 Ho himself would likely object to being labeled a "jazz" musician; in the same essay cited here he rejects the label as a Eurocentric downgrading of Black music. Without getting into the finer points of this argument, the term jazz is used here for the sake of expediency.

10 Fred Wei-han Ho, "Jazz,' Kreolization and Revolutionary Music For the 21st Century', in *Sounding Off: Music as Subversion/Resistance/Revolution*, ed. by Ron Sakolsky and Fred Wei-han Ho (New York: Autonomedia, 1995) p.134.

11 ibid.

How so? In a cultural landscape where every rhythm, every arrangement, is instrumentalized (if you will), how exactly can one compose and combine in a way that undermines that selfsame order? Of course, there is Ho's assertion – a fundamentally sound one – that "even if the performers were simply 'creating' from those experiences, clearly those experiences are contextualized by their social, political, and economic conditions."[12]

Boiling down those conditions to essential features over time and place is, to some degree, counterproductive. Nonetheless, Ho's essay goes in depth into several genres of music, primarily Black music in the American context: blues, jazz, swing. In each case he examines the ways in which certain hallmarks of the genre were picked out and calcified by the culture industry, freezing them in time and made to define the genre with little regard for artists or their histories. Concerns that a genre might prove difficult to package, market, and sell necessitated aesthetic conventions be firmly delineated and frozen in place.

This reification is essential in the process of commodification. As the division of labor deepens, as each practice in everyday life comes under ever greater regimentation, standards are imposed. Notions of taste, of acceptability, of what is "good" or "bad," have a great deal to do with this. That which cannot be standardized, quantified, integrated into a rote and arbitrary arithmetic, is considered less than. It is particularly brazen during the earliest years of popular music, particularly jazz. As Gerhard Kubik writes in *Jazz Transatlantic*:

> [I]n New Orleans at the turn of the twentieth century, the word "music" had a much narrower semantic field than it has nowadays. It

---
12 ibid.

explicitly referred to musical notations. Written scores, i.e., sheet music, were valued highly; it was music as such, and a musician was someone who had learned to read and play from them. Anything else was "fake," including Buddy Bolden's variations on his cornet.[13]

The need to quantify and standardize, to make predictable, and yes, to racialize, essentially segregated different forms of organized and enjoyable sound into "music" and "noise." As styles like ragtime became more popular, the pressures to standardize them came into focus too. Sheet music producers would mark sheets of ragtime songs "coon music" or "Ethiopian two-step."

Even the term "ragtime" carried with it a certain connotation. The then-unpredictable rhythms of ragtime songs sounded, to many western ears, as "ragged," tattered and unfinished. The music's "imperfections" – its improvisations, its moments when the song's beat is seemingly thrown off-balance, different rhythms overlapping in a way unfamiliar to western ears – were, of course, part of its appeal. Still, they had to be measured. Ragtime musicians' polyrhythms, their interlocking beats, were rendered on the page as simple syncopation. As a result, some of the best-known early ragtime – from Scott Joplin's 'Maple Leaf Rag' on down – were notated differently from how they were originally performed. Ultimately, sheet music was incapable of capturing the genre's deeper and intricate characteristics.[14]

A similar process of reification can be found in the history of the famed "blue note." Today it is so essential an ingredient to popular music that we seldom think twice

---

13 Gerhard Kubik, *Jazz Transatlantic, Volume I: The African Undercurrent in Twentieth-Century Jazz Culture* (Jackson: University Press of Mississippi, 2017).p.176.
14 ibid.

about it, heard whenever a singer quavers their voice or a guitarist bends their strings in a solo. But the sound's mere existence, for a time anyway, flummoxed establishment music theorists and critics. Again, the note's "imperfections" – its ambiguity, its ability to blur and exist in the interstitials of a "good" song – were at stake. Again, that which couldn't be understood or quantified was dismissed as noise.

What was the blue note? It could be heard in neither tone nor semitone, the most basic building blocks of western notated music. While contemporary notation systems have figured out ways to signify it, they cannot capture the process of movement within and between these notes: the instability, the insatiability, the sorrow or ribaldry, the somatic earthiness, the emotional locations that cause unease in the straightlaced.

Both the polyrhythm of ragtime and the blue note are but two examples of kreolized sounds that took on enormous socio-political implications. Both are unaccountable musical units, beats and notes that refused to sit still, to behave in the way that social domination demanded of them. In Sartre's terms, they are attempts to fill the gap between the known and the unknown with the intention of the artist, standardizations and blueprints be damned.

Genres that incorporated such musical elements – particularly the blue note – were warned against. Preachers called the blues "devil's music." Members of US Congress would denounce jazz as a style of loose morals, drug use and miscegenation. Radio stations would refuse to play rock and roll songs for fear of juvenile delinquency.

Contested grooves

The processes described by both Ho and Kubik are two different modes of cultural synthesis (both of which are frequently lost in the interminable and imprecise debates around "cultural appropriation"). The first we might call "cultural synthesis from below," driven by the powerless and marginalized in an exploitative system that thrusts people of different backgrounds into the same space. Ho, in his essay, is pointed in declaring kreolization something that can *only* happen from below. To him, synthesis taking place "from above" is necessarily an erasure, a form of cultural imperialism. Kubik's account, of forcing ragtime into a notation system easily understood by the white and western audience, is a good example of this.

Confounding questions remain though. What is it that makes the latter intrinsic to capitalism's cultural method? Why is genuine kreolization, synthesis from below, viewed with such anxiety and suspicion?

What is fundamentally at issue here is a matter of *meaning*. Non-committal, postmodern terms like "pastiche" have instilled in us the idea that two opposite gestures or objects placed together are only that. At best, they create amusing nonsense.

It is a lazy and ahistorical approach. How, if this is the case, do we explain monadic sounds and gestures and styles that came about as the result of hybridization? How to explain the aesthetic that, in combining two or more previous styles, becomes both more genuinely each of its component parts and something else entirely?

When the surrealists, citing Lautréamont, celebrated these juxtapositions, the "chance encounter between a sewing machine and an umbrella on an operating table," they were not just lauding silliness. Rather, they were searching for new languages, new meanings, new modes of thinking that broke with a capitalist rationality that had dragged the European continent into the meat grinder of World War I. In the system's refuse, the flotsam better discarded down the memory hole, they heard – citing Freud – the return of the repressed. That which is left behind, that which polite society would rather forget, still has the potential to disrupt and rewrite its existence.

To the surrealists, freeing human perception of this rationalism was a chance to imagine different, freer modes, a grasp toward revolutionary consciousness. No coincidence then, that most of the first generation of surrealists counted themselves as some form of communist, socialist, or anarchist.[15] Or that they were sincere anti-colonialists, that their movement found a large number of adherents in North Africa, the Caribbean, and across the colonized world. In all these regions, as well as in Europe, surrealist artists and writers looked to the indigenous art of Oceania and the African continent for inspiration and incorporation into their own work.

Kreolization, then, is ill at ease with power. It always, in its purest forms, raises the specter of the anachronized carving out their own space and doing what they wish with their time, that they themselves can choose the activity and emotional states filling their days. How to work. If to work at all. What to make. Who to love. What to think. Where to go. Meaning and subjectivity outside the sanctioned modes of existence.

This is the part of the failure of the attempt to create catch-all musical categories like "world music." In attempting to shove all non-western musics into the same bin – from the Caribbean basin to the Indonesian archipelago, from candomblé to Tuvan throat singing – it

---

15 Salvador Dalí, the fascist-sympathizer who was expelled from the Surrealist International for just that reason, notwithstanding.

attempts to put all of them under the airtight glass of a museum display. Primitive artifacts that must be frozen in time to appreciate them. The evolution of each sound, style, and genre, its movement through time and across place, is denied. Their past is acknowledged, but never their future.

Kreolization presents a challenge to this because it can only happen in the peripheries and interstitials. It necessitates the imagination of a different future, autonomous and free. The rhythms of progress – linear, uninterrupted, monolithic, aiming for the same homogeneity as the gentrified city and the imperial metropole – are complicated by the beats and notes it failed to put to rest and leave behind.

Escape from abstraction

Altogether, it sounds like something not of this Earth. And yet it is profoundly earthy, grounded even as it spirals upwards and outwards. Everything is drenched in echo and reverb, as if the reaches of deep space have been dragged along with it into our ears. The clatter-and-thump of the percussion, the swaggering bassline, the high whine of the horns, and the repetitive jab of the guitars; all of these combine into an experience that circles outward as much as in on itself. As if the cavernous emptiness between beats and notes were thick with some unseen presence. As the track fades out, you are surprised to realize that only four-and-a-half minutes have passed.

This is Jamaican dub legend Lee "Scratch" Perry's 'Black Panta', recorded with his house band the Upsetters and released on the album *Upsetters 14 Black Board Jungle* in 1973. The song's intro makes explicit reference to "the jungle," its title obviously in tribute to the powerful jungle panther. But there is also an obvious double meaning given the timing of the song, in the early 1970s, when the Black Panther movement in the United States and Britain confronted their countries' respective power structures with their vision of Black liberation. By this time anti-colonial rebellion had also swept the African continent, kicking out occupying European powers in several countries like Ghana, Algeria, and Tanzania, inspiring revolutionaries in Perry's native Jamaica and across the Caribbean.

Timing can account for a lot. Surely the release of this song relies on a basic, commonly held knowledge of most listeners. But it is the song's sound, the expansive and other-worldly environment it creates, that allows the listener to reconcile all of these signifiers together: the deep and wild rainforests of the African continent and the Caribbean, the militant Black Panthers organizing in the ghettos of Britain and America, the masses of people on the African continent actively engaged in the remaking of their countries' destinies. There is a natural political affinity conjured up here. In 'Black Panta' they are united aesthetically, an interplay of different histories and futures colliding and growing into something far-reaching and inexorable. As such disparate phenomena can only do beyond the boundaries of time and space where the prosaic rules of causality don't apply. As Luke Ehrlich wrote, "If reggae is Africa in the new world, then dub must be Africa on the moon."[16]

No two songs capture this kind of escape in the same way. Most capture it in dramatically different ways, and plenty fail to capture it entirely. But the very fact that it does exist, that escape not just from a specific place but a mode of time can be given form through music; this

---

16 Luke Ehrlich, 'X-Ray Music: The Volatile History of Dub', in *Reggae Interventional*, ed. by Stephen Davis and Peter Simon (New York: R and B Books, 1982) p.104.

creates a tension with capital's subjugation of music's rhythmic and sonic form.

In turn, this tension forces us to reckon with the way in which Adorno's analysis of popular music falls short. Clearly, his diagnosis provides insight into how the rhythms of commodity production shape the rhythms of popular music. But at best, it only describes one side of the phenomenon, only one dynamic present within it. It fails to grasp that popular music is the result of both top-down and bottom-up processes.

These two countervailing pressures are rarely brought to bear on any song or genre in equal measure. Sometimes it is the bottom-up processes, the free interchange of ideas and sounds among the oppressed and subaltern, that characterizes a style. More frequently in our age it is the top-down, the process of commodification, that predominates in music. At least by the time it gets to the stage of mass consumption.

Whichever side of the tension a song favors, there is at least some degree to which both are always present. Even an artist that has long since left behind their humbler beginnings for the stadium concerts and palatial homes must at least pay lip service to their origins in the dive bars playing for drink tickets.

Further complicating matters is the way in which even the most manufactured and predictable of songs absorbed into the popular consciousness can be reworked and reconfigured by those at society's bottom – quite often without the permission of those who "own" the piece of music. The struggle between copyright and fair use is a reflection of this. So, for that matter, are the attacks on available space – physical and digital – for cheap or free artistic expression.

Stuart Hall in 'Notes On Deconstructing 'the Popular", chronicles this interaction. Counter to Adorno's characterization of popular culture as a one-way tool of social domination, he insists that culture writ large – art, music, sport, literature, media – is one of the ways in which the category of "the people" is defined. Culture and artistic expression reflect back to us a version of ourselves, playing a role in how such categories as "the people," "the working-class," and so on, are constituted. The implied question is who is doing the defining and constituting.

> Sometimes we can be constituted as a force against the power-bloc: that is the historical opening in which it is possible to construct a culture which is genuinely popular. But, in our society, if we are not constituted like that, we will be constituted into its opposite: an effective popular force saying 'Yes' to power. Popular culture is one of the sites where this struggle for and against a culture of the powerful is engaged: it is also the stake to be won or lost in that struggle. It is the arena of consent and resistance.[17]

With this in mind, we might consider the way in which this dialectic plays out within the structure of the music itself as it relates to the psychological state of the artist or listener. In *Groove*, Abel agrees that there is a usefulness in Adorno's approach, but also sees several inconsistencies in it. For one thing, the repetitive rhythms that he criticizes in popular genres are also present in classical genres he writes approvingly of elsewhere. This calls into question whether he is positing an all-encompassing framework for understanding music under capitalism or merely looking for ways to politically criticize

---

17 Stuart Hall, 'Notes On Deconstructing 'the Popular", in *Cultural Resistance Reader*, ed. by Stephen Duncombe (London: Verso, 2002) p.192.

genres he dislikes.

Abel also argues, logically, that the domination of time over the productive process is not a foregone conclusion. For sure, the parcelization of time into identical increments ultimately results in an "abstraction" of time not unlike Lefebvre's abstraction of space, beyond the control of those who inhabit it. But, as virtually every socialist and radical agrees, there still exists the historical potential for working and poor people to exert control over this abstract time – often with the intent of transforming and "un-abstracting" it – rather than allowing it to exert control over them. As Abel remarks in an interview with Kate Bradley:

> Making use of abstract capitalist time has a parallel in the organised working class movement. The first proletarians tried to refuse the tyranny of the clock by being late and skiving. By the late nineteenth century trade unionists had learned that the only way to make gains was to fight the bosses on their own terrain – accepting the discipline of measured time, but using it to fight for a shorter working day.[18]

If this historic potential remains in the realm of work, production, and accumulation, then why would it not in music?

Now music

In 'On the Concept of History', Walter Benjamin posits a way of viewing time and history that refuses to flinch from the disasters of capitalism while also retaining the kernel of revolutionary hope. In the fourteenth thesis,

---

18 Kate Bradley interviewing Mark Abel, 'A Marxist theory of music: It's all in the groove', *RS21* (7 June 2018), https://www.rs21.org.uk/2018/06/17/a-marxist-theory-of-music-its-all-in-the-groove/.

he introduces us to the concept of *jetztzeit*. The German word has no precise English equivalent, but to Benjamin, it is how the revolution regards the passage of time: not as empty or abstract, but full of anarchic potential. As Michael Lowy writes:

> The past contains presentness – *Jetztzeit* – a term variously translated into English as 'now-time' and 'time of the now'. In a variant of Thesis XIV, *Jetztzeit* is defined as an explosive... The aim is to explode the continuum of history with the aim of a conception of historical time that perceives it as 'full', as charged with 'present', explosive, subversive moments. [19]

Modernity, therefore, is a form of society, a temporality, and a mode of being with dual tendencies. It can keep going in the same torpid direction it has taken us, or it can be catapulted in a radically different one. The recapture of abstract time by working and oppressed people reflects this deeply ingrained tension, for they would not have to reclaim anything if they weren't subjugated in the first place. And yet this subjugation inevitably reveals their historic potential to take their time back and place it on a different track.

Abel hears this same "now time" in the structure of groove and popular music. To him, the significance of popular music's rhythmic pattern is that it creates a depth of anticipation. The reception of each beat and note is shaped by the placement of other beats and notes that came directly before. And it is this that creates the possibility for us to assert control over those beats. "Groove deploys a reproduction of an abstract temporal continuum," writes Abel,

---

[19] Michael Lowy, *Fire Alarm: Reading Walter Benjamin's 'On the Concept of History'* (London: Verso, 2016) p.86.

a web of instants, organized hierarchically in relation to a system of time measurement. The effect of such temporal organization, contrary to the accusation of predictability, is to impart a heightened significance to the present, or in practice, to the articulation of each beat of the groove.[20]

The strong associations between the rhythm of popular music and that of commodity then can also be used to thematically undermine the dominance of empty time. Take Pink Floyd's 1973 song 'Money'. The opening bars of this song are of a steady and repetitive bassline, accompanied by the sounds of cash registers opening and coins clinking. But, importantly, though the song is structured around this kind of hypnotic beat, that same beat strays from a neat and predictable format. It is played in an odd time signature of 7/4, producing an unbalanced pattern. Where we think one more note will be, the band instead skips back to the beginning of the musical phrase that has now tricked us.

Though, as Abel notes, odd time signatures are relatively rare in groove/popular music, the case of Money' is the exception that proves the rule. By employing a structure in which there is a "missing note" in an otherwise highly regimented context, Pink Floyd's song exemplifies the way in which the breaking down of life into increments of commensurability also destabilizes our existence. In a way, the dominance of empty time and commodity in popular music is used against itself.

The temporal patterns of popular music, therefore, provide the space and contradiction for us to reimagine those patterns. Moreover, it is difficult to ignore the parallels between a young artist's decision to remake these

---

20 Abel, *Groove*, p.242.

patterns – either digitally or through more analog means – and the bottom-up reclamation of capitalism's productive forces, the transformation of abstract time into a new history.

In these instances even the most overplayed song, a song that has integrated itself into the background of business as usual, can be transformed entirely. Its tempo can be sped up or slowed down to extremes. The details of its syncopations and polyrhythms can be adjusted to make the beat's anatomy unrecognizable. The contradictions that brought about the present moment provide just enough space to smash them together and provide a route of radical escape.

Grime redemption

In the video for Skepta's 2014 single 'That's Not Me', the grime MC uses a rewired pair of headphones as a microphone. This is a not uncommon practice, reflecting grime's deep connection with London's pirate radio scene. Still, it is difficult to imagine a more pointed symbolism. Contrasted with Mark Fisher's "OedIpod consumer bliss," Skepta takes an instrument that musically entrenches the condition of urban isolation and arrhythmia, and literally turns it inside out.

The music also sounds, in its own way, turned inside out. The aggressive digital percussion and the bass are processed and reprocessed and filtered and re-filtered to such an extreme degree that they threaten to buzz the sides of the speakers right off. The keys sound as if they have been hijacked internally, made organically into their own by embracing their own imprecision and decay.

Among other themes, the track's lyrics feature a specific rejection of conspicuous consumption. Skepta rejects the trappings of luxury that are seemingly so ubiquitous elsewhere in music: "Yeah, I used to wear Gucci / Put it all in the bin 'cause that's not me." This comes off not so much as placing himself on a moral highground next to other MC's, but rather as an expression of a more authentic sense of self and individual creative desire.

We also see, in the video's background, crudely underlaying footage of Skepta, footage of the Meridian Estates, the public housing complex in Tottenham, North London where Skepta was raised by Nigerian immigrant parents. Against the shiny swirl of London the global financial center, 'That's Not Me' recontextualizes and celebrates the crude, the rough, and the neglected. What sounds like noise to privileged ears is here turned into a new sonic paradigm that is pointedly not for the privileged.

'That's Not Me' was something of a watershed for grime music. The album it eventually appeared on, *Konnichiwa*, won Britain's coveted Mercury Music Prize in September of 2016. But before this, grime had spent years hounded to music's margins. After its initial popularity in the early 2000s, London's grime scene found itself the target of the city's government and law enforcement.

New ordinances were passed requiring clubs to submit Form 696, described euphemistically as a "live music risk assessment." The suggestion from the London Metropolitan Police was that this was to ensure the safety of live performances themselves; if the form wasn't turned in or filled out correctly, then the police would force the event to cancel. In fact, even when promoters filled out the forms properly, the cops might still shut them down. Original versions of the form, in use until 2008, asked which racial and ethnic groups were likely to show up at the event. In essence, social and creative spaces were being regulated and cracked down on, if not shut down entirely. Grime in particular was forced back underground.

But then, this wasn't exactly new for working-class communities of colour in Britain. Dan Hancox, in *Inner City Pressure*, explicitly ties grime's initial gestation to the "modernization" of the welfare state and urban life generally, spearheaded by Tony Blair's New Labour government. This was the time when CCTV cameras were going in on every corner of the city, when Anti-Social Behaviour Orders (ASBOs) were introduced, and when billions of pounds were being poured into "urban regeneration" projects that pushed poor, working-class people out of their homes. State subsidies that made it possible for artists of humbler origins to survive, that kept community arts and music spaces open, were also scrapped. "The grime kids went without those state subsidies," Hancox writes.

> For all that we should celebrate their independent, DIY spirit and sheer self-motivated perseverance – teenagers with nothing, making something more dazzling and millennial-modern than anyone could have ever imagined – they did so with the help of youth clubs, school teachers, and a collective, communitarian spirit that was being pummelled by a government determined to dismantle it, in the name of remaking the inner city.[21]

Even the genre's name, grime, caught on because it raised images of what a gentrifying London would rather get rid of. As Hancox writes, there is a dose of Christian moralism when city governments speak of "regeneration," as if anything rough around the edges, anything

---

21 Dan Hancox, *Inner City Pressure: The Story of Grime* (London: William Collins, 2018) p.30.

that doesn't fit into the linear progress of the city as a site of accumulation, is bound to be vice-ridden and morally compromised. Grime, in drumming up images of dirt and filth, rubbed respectable London's face in everything it wanted out of sight and mind (though the connotations were also enough for many among grime's original generation to voice opposition to the label).

The presence of residential spaces, publicly maintained but increasingly neglected, not just in 'That's Not Me' but in grime generally, is less a stylistic choice than a necessity. Building on Cynthia Cruz's earlier remark, domestic spaces are oftentimes the only space a poor or working-class artist can safely create. The artist, made invisible virtually everywhere else, takes advantage of what little space they have to make their time bearable, less homogenous, leading somewhere other than a future that doesn't exist. The site of survival becomes a site of creative escape. Which must tell us something about the role of creativity in survival.

Building on Sartre and translating the former's ideas about radical subjectivity into explicitly anti-racist and anti-colonial terms, Frantz Fanon's work sought to chart a path along which the subjugated might go "from object to subject." To disrupt the deeply ingrained assumptions of inferiority that surrounded them, the subject must recognize their own ontological power, their potential to recreate the world in their image. If achieving this kind of dignity and self-worth "implies restructuring the world," as Fanon insists, then so too does it imply restructuring the pace at which life is lived, forcing time to turn around and reckon with the humanity of those otherwise rendered faceless.[22]

---

22 Frantz Fanon, *Black Skin, White Masks* [1952], trans. Richard Philcox (New York: Grove Press, 2007), and Peter Hudis, *Frantz Fanon: Philosopher of the Barricades* (London: Pluto Press, 2015).

Songs like 'That's Not Me' are, therefore, a redemption of the anachronized played out in sonic form. And it is the anachronized, those exiled from history, who are in a particular position to disrupt it. "Anachronisms can disturb the homogeneous linear time of capitalism and the nation-state," writes Massimiliano Tomba, "and can orient the trajectory of political modernity in a different direction."[23]

It is the atomic unit of kreolization. Here, at its most authentic, we hear not only a mode representing the influences, beliefs, and experiences of one narrative remade to suit those of another, but the deliberately scrapped and forgotten coming back into history's center stage, repurposing and making itself un-ignorable. If music is the aestheticization of time, then the artist's re-astheticization of time stands in for the potential to master time, and history, for our own. Music's utopian impulse comes close to being actualized here. Close, but not quite.

---

[23] Massimiliano Tomba, 'Deprovincializing Marx: On Harry Harootunian's Reading of Marx', *Viewpoint Magazine* (27 June 2017) https://viewpointmag.com/2017/06/27/deprovincializing-marx-on-harry-harootunians-reading-of-marx/.

Part Three
Anachronism, Attack

> "Cities, like dreams, are made of desires and fears, even if the thread of their discourse is secret, their rules are absurd, their perspectives deceitful and everything conceals something else."
> Italo Calvino, *Invisible Cities*

> "We are bodies responding differently, a (total) force, like against you. You react to push it, re-create it. Resist it. It is the opposite pressure producing (in this case) the sound, the music."
> LeRoi Jones (Amiri Baraka), 'The Changing Same'

Music as liberated space

When people show you who they are, you should believe them the first time. The same goes for architecture. Directly abutting the hub of British political power, London's Parliament Square intends to project an aura that is consciously steeped in its own imperial past, as well as

Britain's existence as one of the most durable monarchies in modern history. The pretense is one above and outside of time itself.

But it is also, after all, *Parliament* Square. As such there is a clear attempt to connote democratic purchase. The stately, stuffy, and straight-laced Palace of Westminster that houses Britain's Parliament to the square's east is intended to be counterbalanced by the large, flat, grassy field itself, a space where power is ostensibly leveled.

Except that Westminster isn't the only house of immense power bordering Parliament Square. To the north are the buildings of Whitehall, housing the administrative center of Britain's executive. To the west is Middlesex Guildhall, frequent headquarters of the Supreme Court. And to the south is Westminster Abbey, one of the most important cathedrals in the Church of England, and where most members of the Royal Family are wed. If Parliament Square is intended as a space of gathering, then the ornate towers surrounding it are where the gathering stops.

In 1868, during the urban redesign that created the square, traffic lights were installed on the surrounding roads. These were the first traffic lights in history, intended to relieve congestion in what was then the world's largest and most densely populated city.

Since then, several statues of Britain's most iconic legislators have been installed: Winston Churchill, Benjamin Disraeli, Robert Peel, David Lloyd George, and others who have shepherded and maintained the empire. The inclusion of those who fought for some basic freedoms in history – Millicent Fawcett, Abraham Lincoln, Nelson Mandela – might perhaps signify some form of modernization, a decision to take a different, more enfranchised path. But the endurance of the statue of Jan Smuts – second Prime Minister of South Africa and a primary architect of the apartheid regime, installed at Churchill's initiative and surviving despite decades of protest – is a reminder that what was will always be.

The 21st century has seen several legal battles over who may use Parliament Square and for what purposes. Historically, Parliament Square has been a gathering place for demonstrations. The 2005 Serious Organised Crime and Police Act banned gatherings in the square that had not received prior authorization from the London Metropolitan Police Commissioner. This was partially repealed in 2011, though vague reference to "prohibited activities" left the door open to repression.

In other words, Parliament Square is a prime example of how the city of late capitalism can defang protest through its permission and containment. Absolute freedoms are nowhere here, but narrow allowance of gathering, movement, and speech are disguised as them. It is a space of chance and encounter, yes, but necessarily limited chance and controlled encounter, leaving the line of Great British history intact. If the traffic lights aren't a reminder of this, then the statues and ornamental architecture certainly are.

On December 9th 2010, these parameters were, however briefly and in unlikely circumstances, smashed. Over several days, protests against the ruling Conservative-Liberal Democrat coalition's education "reforms" had grown in size and militancy. Spearheaded by Prime Minister David Cameron – blue-blooded Oxfordian with a predilection for pigs – the proposed changes increased the all-around price of higher education in Britain. Government subsidies were removed, and fee caps raised, effectively making university unobtainable for many poor and working-class youth.

Media maligned protesters as privileged undergraduates play-acting revolution. In actuality, the demonstrations included a large presence from some of

London's poorest neighborhoods: Tower Hamlets, Croydon, the housing estates in Islington and other areas. These were "the EMA kids," who could not afford to take up further education without help from the Education Maintenance Allowance, a weekly stipend designed to keep poorer kids in school, which was now on the government's chopping block.

Demonstrators had already shown themselves willing to cross the geographical boundaries of safe, "accepted" protest a few weeks earlier. On November 10th, they broke through police lines, then the front doors of 30 Millbank, occupying the campaign headquarters of the Conservative Party. For a few hours, this smooth-faced skyscraper overlooking the River Thames had its unflappable façade punctured by the controlled chaos of spirited, militant movement.

December 9th was the day that the government's reforms passed. Two mass marches were called in in London, organized by anti-cuts and student groups but also backed by trade unions and the organized left. Both were large, young, and incredibly angry.

The events of the day have by now been immortalized in countless articles and books, but the broad strokes are a stunning example of how insurgent peoples can reshape space through time – and the role that music has in it. At around 2:30pm, marchers reached Parliament Square and broke through the police barricades. Hundreds flooded the square. Some lit placards and other debris on fire, others climbed up lampposts to lead chants. At least one protester had the simple yet brilliant idea to spray-paint on the grass, in massive pink letters, big enough for news helicopters to pick up: "NO."[1]

---
[1] Sequence of events verified through day-of coverage, *Guardian*: https://www.theguardian.com/education/blog/2010/dec/09/student-protests-live-coverage.

ANACHRONISM, ATTACK

That is what this was: an exercise in mass negation. Elsewhere in central London, any sign of privilege was similarly set upon by protesters, including the Rolls Royce of Prince Charles and Camilla Parker-Bowles – with the royals still inside. By nightfall, the hundreds in Parliament Square had swelled to thousands. Despite attempts to kettle the protesters, the Metropolitan Police had lost whatever tenuous control they might have previously had. Several people, on both the side of the police and the protesters, had been injured (though proportionately many more protesters than cops).

Windows on the front of the HM Customs and Revenue building on the square's east side were smashed. Same on the opposite side of the square at the Supreme Court, where someone spraypainted Guy Debord's inspired slogan: "Be realistic – demand the impossible."[2]

As fires burned in the square, black-clad youth blasted loud and abrasive music over a sound system. They danced and flailed and grabbed each other round the neck, embracing each other against the real futureless future that came down that night. A certain nihilism was not only inevitable, but wholly defensible. For that night, young people who spent much of their lives being told that the whole of history was beyond their grasp acted on their own terms, filled their night with their presence, and forced the world to acknowledge it.

The music that filled Parliament Square that night was mislabeled not once, but twice. First, Paul Mason called the protests "the dubstep rebellion." He was quickly corrected on social media by people who were present, who also included a playlist. Turns out not many tracks played could be reasonably labeled "dubstep." The next day, a corrective was floated: "the grime rebellion."

---

2 Paul Mason, *Why It's Still Kicking off Everywhere: The New Global Revolutions* (London: Verso, 2013) p.15.

Though, as Dan Hancox also pointed out, there wasn't much grime on that playlist either.[3]

Rather, the songs played were quite eclectic, representing a broad cross-section of rap, R&B, and other offshoot genres from both sides of the pond. There was Rihanna in there, as well as 50 Cent. Jamaican dancehall was represented with Elephant Man's 'Bun Bad Mind' and Vybz Kartel's 'Ramping Shop'. The influence of dance genres like drum & bass and UK garage could be heard too.

And yes, there was one track that counted as dubstep: a collaboration between Croydon-based producer Benga, and Coki of the duo Digital Mystikz. Imagining Benga & Coki's 'Night' playing in Parliament Square that night, its beeping instrumentation and sparse skitter-step beats wafting between buildings and statues that once stood impregnable but now were covered with graffiti, the light of bonfires bouncing off them, gives us a good sense of the dramatic contrast between what the space was and what it had turned into.

Truth be told, it does appear that grime held a special place that night. Included on the playlist was "Serious," by Skepta's little brother and frequent collaborator JME. But Lethal Bizzle's 'Pow! (Forward)' seems to capture the massive and radical change inherent in that moment. Released in 2004 (and not to be confused with its sequel tracks 'Forward Riddim 2' or 'Pow 2011'), it featured guest appearances from no fewer than nine other underground grime MCs, all of them rapping in the quick and furious style distinctive of the genre. Like the lyrics and their delivery, the beat is frenetic and unrelenting, slapping and punching its way through whatever might wander in front of it. Banned from several British

---

3 Dan Hancox, 'This is Our Riot: "POW!"', (10 December 2010), http://dan-hancox.blogspot.com/2010/12/this-is-our-riot-pow.html.

radio stations and clubs because of its "controversial" lyrical references to gun culture, it nonetheless managed to become a favorite in the grime scene and came very close to puncturing the UK top ten.

'Pow!' is a final warning at the last minute. According to Hancox, it was played three times in a row that night. By the next morning, the protests had dispersed, and within a matter of days Parliament Square was back to its orderly self, its paternal statues quietly approving of the patterned traffic that came and went, so that London might continue to function in its role of global financial hub. But on the night of December 9th, it was equal parts dancefloor and temporary autonomous zone, a place where the marginalized and anachronized pushed themselves, albeit symbolically, into the center of British power. What had once been a place where the trajectory of time was shepherded unperturbed through history was transformed into a site of radical rupture. A very different future – rough-and-ready, anarchic-and-free – was evident.

Groove heterotopia

Ideally, mass spaces of shared artistic liberation should not only be in existence, but easily accessible. They should also, just as crucially, be permanent sites of dialogue and exchange, not just in and of themselves but in the context of the city. If a certain vision of the world can be hammered out within its confines, it should also be able to share it beyond. These are cultural spaces that exact a certain kind of soft (and occasionally not-so-soft) democratic power.

Henri Lefebvre has a name for these kinds of spaces: "heterotopia." Defined as "spaces of difference," heterotopia is neither the soulless and abstracted space designed to isolate us, nor the proposed "concrete utopia" that negates it. It is a space somewhere in between, of dynamism and contingency, of futures in flux as activated denizens realize their ability to change the world around them. As David Harvey summarizes in *Rebel Cities*, "Lefebvre's concept of heterotopia… delineates liminal social spaces of possibility where 'something different' is not only possible, but fundamental for the defining of revolutionary trajectories."[4]

Whether public or private or somewhere in between, they exist outside of the full gaze of the increasingly surveilled, authoritarian city. As such, they allow for alternative subjectivities to be discovered and nurtured. Working-class restaurants and bars, independent community spaces, parks forgotten or infrequently observed by authorities, squatted residences. There is, as Harvey says, the strong potential for revolutionary visions to be forged in these liminal spaces. There is also a profound instability inherent in them. Particularly as the authoritarian city has, through privatization or repression, either eliminated these places, or made them inaccessible.

Alas, very few exist. Even fewer can shape themselves through the creativity of their participants into something radical and free, never mind go beyond the confines of their own walls. Neoliberal austerity has shuttered most of these spaces, hobbled the rest, and erased the very idea that they are a democratic right. Therefore, the creation of truly free space and time is necessarily in opposition to the designed rhythms of the authoritarian city. Heterotopia, if it is to survive, must push itself from the margins into the city's center, into its impregnable citadels.

Perhaps therefore, when oppressed people create their own scenes and spaces, their own cultural and

---

[4] Harvey, *Rebel Cities*, p.xvii.

musical expressions, it necessarily involves, on some level, a challenge to its environment, urban or otherwise. During the earliest days of hip-hop in the Bronx, DJs bringing their parties outside would jimmy open streetlights as a power source for their turntables. Grime itself, in its own origin years, greatly relied on pirate radio stations set up by youth in the housing estates, bringing their mixing equipment and transistors up to the top of the tower blocks to be heard by anyone who was tuned to the right frequency. The rhythms of survival, shoved into the cracks the homogenized city cannot plaster over, continue to emerge, and reach other ears.

Then there are the moments when these rhythms push out from the cracks, when they seize enough of the popular imagination to bring them out of the shadows, and for the sounds they bring with them to inhabit the city in such a way that everything about it feels different.

This, according to many who participated in it, was endemic in the rise of that broad array of sounds and scenes we now generally refer to as "rave." It's not a particularly specific designation, ascribed to virtually every genre of electronic dance music from Detroit techno to British big beat, from the acid house of Phuture to the atmospheric drum and bass of LTJ Bukem. Nor are these genres the only ones capable of interacting with space in such a way. What all had in common, though, was a very specific arrangement of rhythm and sound that both emerged from and bristled against a spatial politic that defined the formative decades of neoliberalism.

The shuttering of factories in the 1980s and 90s, along with general urban disinvestment, left a great deal of disused space. It also left people searching for a sense of hope that neither economics nor politics could provide. This was abandonment and anachronization on a mass scale. It was no coincidence that these scenes were profoundly multi-racial, often queer-friendly, sampling, repurposing and deepening the influences of funk, soul, and disco. DJs like Frankie Knuckles – Black, gay, born in the intense neglect of the Bronx – were able to thrive here. In this setting, between a present shaped like emptiness and a future that deserved to be better, something like raves – and the countless tracks that animated them – were bound to take shape.

Take, for example, the Detroit techno scene. At its height in the 1990s, its epicenter was the Packard Plant. This was an automobile plant opened in 1903 and shuttered in 1957, leaving three and a half million feet of indoor space unused. Other more recently abandoned spaces – warehouses, machine shops – were in the surrounding area. Spaces that once echoed with the steady and constant pound of the assembly line or the rapid pace of shipping and receiving now stood still as capital found other, more efficient places to reproduce itself. And, not by any coincidence, the same economic downturn that had muted these spaces had also brought a palpable anxiety and desperation to the surrounding residential neighborhoods. Though Detroit techno's earliest artists arrived not from the inner cities but from the Black middle-class suburbs, the preoccupation with creating a future in what had been discarded and left behind was clear enough.[5]

Many accounts of Detroit techno refer to its sound as "futuristic," and some of its originators explicitly associated it with the ideas of Afrofuturism. There was a fascination with the possibility of digital recording and sampling. The instrumentation used – Roland synthesizers, drum machines, and of course turntables – were together able to create sound combinations never heard

---

5 Arthur Bray, 'The Golden Years – Detroit Techno's Warehouse Scene', *Maekan* (3 July 2018), https://maekan.com/story/the-golden-years-detroit-technos-warehouse-scene/.

before. Beats could be sped up or slowed down at will. The brassy sound of a harpsichord could be manipulated and distorted into something more akin to an overdriven guitar. Or the notes could take on a timbre unrecognizable to those more familiar with traditional instruments, like something from another planet entirely, sparkling-beeping sounds skipping through the night sky down to the earth you stood on.

The performances that gestated these kinds of sounds also existed largely, especially in those early days, without permission. By the '90s, the Packard Plant had stood empty for so long that few artists or attendees really knew who even owned the shell that stood in its place. Nor did they really care. On those nights, it belonged to all of them. The reach of sound systems would be extended by the plant's caverns, inhabited by thousands of people hoping for an experience defined by unity and freedom. New temporal arrangements gave the space a different feel. Depressive stillness was replaced by the energy of thousands of bodies moving separately to the same time – a time they both carried and were carried by. It wasn't uncommon for those in attendance to catch the sunrise in disbelief that the night was over.

Though the myriad subgenres that could be loosely lumped together as "rave music" came to exhibit these kinds of characteristics in vastly different ways, the characteristics themselves were constant. Repetitive beats, harmonies and melodies that created near-hypnotic states in both creator and listener. The use of digital technologies could, within this specific rubric, locate just about any previously made sound and create something new from it – though it does bear mentioning that many subgenres were far from averse to including live guitars, bass, drums or keyboards in their performances, evidenced in artists as different as the Happy Mondays and Prodigy.

Finally, performances required, invited, and necessitated, mass participation. Listening to these sounds on headphones or with your friends in a living room was all well and good, but the spontaneity and mass energy of performance, thousands of people like you moved by the same sounds, was where the music really came alive. The heights of these scenes – be they in Detroit or Manchester, Rotterdam or Goa – relied on these kinds of performances. Music as event and encounter.

Abel, in *Groove* touches on the experience this kind of ecumenical rhythm creates in its listeners and participants. Referencing late musicologist Christopher Small, he highlights music as a process rather than an object. The act of music making in the presence of others dissolves the boundary between inner and outer, between individual and collective. As Abel writes:

> The notion that the practice of 'musicking,' to use Christopher Small's neologism, involves the synchronisation of the subjective time consciousness of all those participating – composers, performers, and listeners alike – into a vivid present which has its roots in objective physical activity in the outer world, seems to chime with our experience of enjoying music.[6]

In other words, the experience of a shared rhythm is one of shared sensitization. Not only is the inner world of our imagination externalized, the irreal projections of the mind made into something perceivable, it is made into a collective touchstone. It seizes each of our highly subjective "internal clocks," and puts them on a common wavelength, a shared aestheticization of time.

---

6 Abel, *Groove*, p.143.

ANACHRONISM, ATTACK

Dangerous beats and psychedelic reason

In *Energy Flash*, his exhaustive retelling of the history of rave music and dance culture, Simon Reynolds describes the massive and infamous 1992 Castlemorton Common Festival as "a scene weirdly poised between idyllic and apocalyptic." Castlemorton took place not in any city center but in the rural Malvern Hills district of Worchestershire, England (a testament to just how popular raves had become if the only place suitable for the largest ones weren't abandoned factories but massive open fields). Nonetheless, this characterization seems a fitting description for the rave scene. Sites left to decay and warp the lives of those who depended on them were chaotically remade into freer versions themselves.

That much of this was aided with the use of psychoactive or hallucinogenic substances – marijuana, LSD, MDMA – certainly earned the umbrage of polite society. But it also speaks to the state of mind that participants tried to achieve, not just through altered consciousness but shared rhythm and, consequentially, *shared consciousness*, transcending the doldrums of work and the stultifying sameness of commodity.

Building on Herbert Marcuse and borrowing the term from Mark Fisher, Matt Colquhoun posits the term "psychedelic reason," distinguishing the term from so many frivolous and empty-headed connotations that today come with something deemed "psychedelic."

> It is the dormant *function* of psychedelia, in this sense, rather than its familiar aesthetic form, that remains relevant to us in the present moment: the way the word itself, all aesthetic associations aside, connotes the manifestation of what is deep within the mind, not simply on its surface. An irregular conjunction

of the modern English prefix "psyche" and the more blatant Greek root "*dēlos*" — meaning "manifest" or "reveal" — the psychedelic is that which manifests what is in the mind, echoing Marx's Spinozist adage, once again, that we must not settle for interpreting the world but instead strive to change it.[7]

Though it would be an exaggeration to ascribe this kind of consciousness to the rave scene *tout court*, the kernel of it is evident. The drugs certainly helped, but it was just as much the collective elation of shared rhythm and transcendent sonic dynamics, the falling away of ego, the approach toward something like what the hippies called "one-ness." In such an environment, it was likely easy to imagine the walls of the club, the warehouse, the auto plant, repurposed, perhaps even disappearing entirely, in favor of something that made life more fulfilling.

Celebration of this space and time, this carnivalesque atmosphere, should not be uncritical or unqualified. Participants may point to plenty of instances in which such spaces proved unsafe for women, non-binary and queer people, and people of color. These should not be taken lightly, and efforts by scene members to make them safe supported. Particularly because the entire ethos of psychedelic reason, of reimagining relations with ourselves, each other, and the glimpse of a world beyond subjugation, flies in the face of such bigotry, racism, and misogyny.

It has been said that the establishment feared nothing more in the 1960s than working class people becoming

---

7 Matt Colquhoun, 'Introduction', in Mark Fisher, *Postcapitalist Desire: The Final Lectures* (London: Repeater, 2021) p.14.

hippies.[8] One gets the feeling that they thought the same thing about the rave scene. In the United States, the focus of the war on drugs pivoted to whip up public outcry over drug use at illegal raves. Police in Chicago began banning after-hours parties and revoking venues' liquor licenses. Those who defied the ban were raided. Same in New York, Detroit, and other cities.

In Britain, tabloids shrieked of ecstasy dealers and acid freaks wantonly luring the youth of England into drugged-out depravity. "Crazed Acid Mob Attack Police" screamed the *News of the World*. "Acid Raid Cops Flee 3000 At Party," declared the *Sun*, "Drug Pushers Carry On." The impression was one of a scene threatening the very fabric of a decent society, the ravers' idyll an unstable vortex of apocalypse so powerful it can disarm the police.

Other raids were more successful. In the 1990s, it was the London Metropolitan Police's Territorial Support Group breaking up the largest parties. As former raver and writer Tim Guest pointed out, the TSG also used to break up protests at the G20 summit held in the city in 2009. At its climax, the campaign against raves even saw helicopters hovering over the city to escort sound system rigs out of London.

After Castlemorton, Members of Parliament introduced bills explicitly targeting rave culture. The Criminal Justice and Public Order Act of 1994 had a section that outlawed outdoor parties, specifically singling out those that played music that "includes sounds wholly or predominantly characterised by the emission of a succession

---

8 The observation is made by Matt Colquhoun in the introduction to *Postcapitalist Desire*. While glib, it points to the potential of what might have happened had the anti-work philosophy of the counterculture fully encountered and combined with what at the time was a growing militancy and rebelliousness among industrial workers in the US and GB.

of repetitive beats." Groups of ten or more people who publicly congregated to attend these parties could be subject to arrest and imprisonment.

Ravers were not the only scene targeted by the Criminal Justice Act. In its far-reaching attempt to tighten the government's grip on public and urban space, the bill revoked local councils' duty to provide space for Travellers and itinerant groups, increased legal penalties for squatters, and loosened restrictions on police stop and search. Little wonder then that the Criminal Justice Act provoked large protests, drawing tens of thousands into London in May, July, and October of 1994. The first two ended in massive outdoor raves. The last was met with heavy police violence.

The repression of the rave scene forced it to draw broader political conclusions. These conclusions were not wholly separate from the scene's aesthetic and cultural principles. For many ravers, the deep feelings of freedom and abandon they had internalized could not be let go. It wasn't just the intoxication of the feeling itself, the allure of psychedelic reason, but the fact that if the bill succeeded, all that would be left were the dull, repetitive patterns of working life. Get up, go to work, come home, repeat; and remember to avoid eye contact at all costs.

"The loss of control, the fear of alternative lifestyles, a desire to drive MDMA-taking youth back to revenue-creating alcohol and the huge untapped business opportunity presented by the illegal party scene have all been touted as factors behind the crackdown of 1994," writes Frankie Mullin.[9] It was similarly impossible to ignore the dimensions of race and racism at play. Most raves were multiracial, making it difficult to gloss over

---

9 Frankie Mullin, 'How UK Ravers Raged Against the Ban', *Vice* (15 July 2014), https://www.vice.com/en/article/vd8gbj/anti-rave-act-protests-20th-anniversary-204.

the simultaneous criminalization of non-white ethnic groups that the Criminal Justice Act sought to codify.

The repression and resistance also meant that ravers and artists would begin to hear the music in a very different way. Likewise for the place of that music in history. "One of the interesting things about the scene is that you did get these... middle-class ravers who would set up techno sound systems in an abandoned railway arch, and all of a sudden be in confrontation with the police," said Anindya Bhattacharya, a London-based activist and DJ. "And that would be a very, very rapidly politicizing experience. And they'd suddenly realize about this history of Black music and Black culture and why people rioted. It was quite interesting to see how quickly people picked up on this."

A million deflected futures

Exact dates of rave's decline vary, but it seems fair to generally place in the first decade of the 21st century. By then, a whole generation had grown up under the constant chorus that society didn't exist, and even if it did, it didn't owe us anything. The victory of the '94 Criminal Justice Act, the subsequent migration of raves into "legitimate" clubs that could be better monetized, while still incubating some good artists, also seemed to tame the flourishing subgenres that gave the scene such diversity and vibrant energy.

In *Pitchfork*, Reynolds looks back on electronic artist Burial's album Untrue, released ten years earlier. By the time *Untrue* was released, the CCTV cameras and ASBO's, the police raids and shuttering of semi-legal clubs, had done the trick. What had once provided youth a site of exploration and togetherness had been fractured and scattered to the wind.

As Reynolds writes, Burial's music – often referred to as "post-dubstep" – channels a tragically rediscovered isolation. *Untrue*, undoubtedly Burial's masterpiece, is filled with lonely, echoing percussions, longing sampled instrumentations, human voices manipulated to their most eerie and inhuman, and densely implanted sounds often so faint that they can only work on our subconscious. There is a sense of mourning on *Untrue*, the subtle, stinging tinge of resentment running underneath.

Citing Fisher, Reynolds writes that Burial's music is:

> A misty-eyed memorial to the British subculture of pirate radio and warehouse raves that coalesced at the end of the '80s, evolved through mutant '90s styles like jungle and 2-step garage, then splintered into 21st century offshoots like grime and dubstep. Listening to [Burial's self-titled debut album] *Burial*, Fisher wrote, felt "like walking into the abandoned spaces once carnivalized by raves and finding them returned to depopulated dereliction. Muted air horns flare like the ghosts of raves past."[10]

Burial – later revealed to be a young South Londoner named William Bevan – was, it turns out, a bit too young to have participated in the rave scene at its height. According to him, he was introduced to jungle and garage music by his older brothers. Nonetheless, the sense of loss is so deep in his work, particularly *Untrue*, that he very clearly understands what was lost when as the scene began to dissolve.

---

10 Simon Reynolds, 'Why Burial's *Untrue* is the Most Important Electronic Album of the Century So Far', *Pitchfork* (26 October 2017), https://pitchfork.com/features/article/why-burials-untrue-is-the-most-important-electronic-album-of-the-century-so-far/.

ANACHRONISM, ATTACK

It was, after all, not just the massive parties that had faded. So had much of the social stability that had allowed youth culture to flourish in the first place. In its place was a literal nothing. The "flexibilities" that were supposed to lead to new opportunities unfettered by regulation and restraint had instead led to precarity, isolation, and a mental-health epidemic so overwhelming that it literally has us feeling that the floor has disappeared. An existence in non-existence.

What gives music like Burial's such resonance is its reminder that, through the fractured nothing, there once indeed was a something. And, in some splintered, refracted way, it is still there. Even if all attempts to grab it are illusory, even if the future it represented never came to fruition, it still might have at one point. Is that a future still worth indulging? Can it be brought from memory into actual, concrete reality?

There is a name for all this, first coined by Jacques Derrida, further fleshed out by Fisher: *Hauntology*. Since Fisher's death in 2017 the term has become widely used and cited, even giving rise to a loose ecosystem of "hauntology studies" among vaguely punky critical theorists. It is a term that has taken hold because it manages to capture a specific kind of ennui that grips young (and, increasingly, not-so-young) working-class people in the 21st century. Particularly its more marginalized denizens. Increasingly, just as we are the ones haunted by futures that never came, so too are we the ones doing the actual haunting.

Since the release of *Untrue*, Burial's music – released through a long string of singles and EPs – has become more abstract, more presently absent and absently present. Often, his songs have eschewed even a basic beat, their own rhythmic unmooring reflecting our own as memories of past hopes grow smaller and smaller in the rearview mirror. And yet, there always persists – obscured and refracted though it may be – something begging us to hold it, even if it cannot be touched. This kernel of futurity within is enough to make us ask whether it might take root today, however unlikely. Even in despair, the imagination searches for a future.

Demonstration and redefinition

Writing at the height of the uprisings of 1968, socialist and art critic John Berger considered demonstrations from the aesthetic angle. Rather than cordon off the aesthetic from the material and political, he looked at mass protest through the most basic prism of time and space. In so doing, he put his finger on the entire reason demonstrations are, notwithstanding so many attempts to render them ineffective set-pieces, a worthwhile endeavor.

Importantly, Berger both distinguishes the mass demonstration from the riot or revolutionary uprising and mentions that the former may become one of the latter two. Berger refers to mass demonstrations as "rehearsals for revolution." He elaborates:

> The demonstration, an irregular event created by the demonstrators, nevertheless takes place near the city centre, intended for very different uses. The demonstrators interrupt the regular life of the streets they march through or of the open spaces they fill. They cut off these areas, and, not yet having the power to occupy them permanently, they transform them into a temporary stage on which they dramatise the power they still lack.
>
> The demonstrators' view of the city

surrounding their stage also changes. By demonstrating, they manifest a greater freedom and independence – a greater creativity, even although the product is only symbolic – than they can ever achieve individually or collectively when pursuing their regular lives. In their regular pursuits they only modify circumstances; by demonstrating they symbolically oppose their very existence to circumstances.[11]

We might also extend this analysis beyond what the demonstration makes appear, and into what it wills into sonic existence. Virtually every demonstration includes the use of chants, of rhythm, often of song too. Streets and sidewalks that are designed to siphon people and cars at a relatively quick clip are flooded with a number of human bodies not anticipated by their planners. Synchronized sound bounces off tall buildings intended to shelter their inhabitants from the consequence of the outside world, pulling them to the window to observe. Space is transformed through the mass creation of alternative time.

It is not altogether unlike the height of the rave scene, also often inhering a kind of utopian departure. Only now, it takes aim at transforming more than just a disused warehouse or abandoned underpass. Those who haunted at the city's edge now push their way into the center of the city and its collective imagination.

Quite often, in doing so, it is also the rhythm, the music itself, that is transformed. A chant is meaningless if its words remain written on the page or memorized in the marchers' heads. They are given substantive meaning in their mass enunciation. A dramatically different context, collectively created, can change the meaning of

---

[11] John Berger, 'The Nature of Mass Demonstrations', *New Society* (23 May 1968), https://www.marxists.org/history/etol/newspape/isj/1968/no034/berger.htm.

the song itself.

During the 1967 urban rebellion in Detroit – an uprising against police violence and the substandard social conditions experienced by the city's Black community – some protesters dragged their stereo speakers to the roof of buildings to blast Martha and the Vandellas' 'Dancing in the Street'. Martha Reeves' objection to her song's reappropriation – "My lord, it was a party song!" – came too little, too late. By that time, H. Rap Brown and other Black militants had started to replay the song at demonstrations. Its lyrics, originally as innocuous as any other feel-good Motown song, had come to mean something else: that the feelings of urban militancy, of taking back control of one's surroundings, could be cut from the same cloth as celebration.

It's here that we should revisit Walter Benjamin, the surrealists, and the situationists. It is one thing to redefine on an individual level, to place an umbrella next to a sewing machine, a distorted sound filter over a previously clean rhythm. It is another to do so on a mass level, collectively. Blasting Reeves' song from the rooftops as rioters and protesters battled with the National Guard below is a remarkable example of what the situationists called *détournement*. This was the deliberate redefinition of mainstream culture to essentially turn its meaning inside out. Though the situationists primarily practiced this through the medium of visual art – rewriting or otherwise recontexualizing magazine advertisements to undermine them – it can also very well be applied to music. The example of Detroit shows that it can be done quite organically; one does not need to be steeped in the situationist theory of *détournement* to practice it.

This also points to the gap – indeed the outright conflict – between the temporality of what Debord termed "the society of the spectacle" and the temporality of fully actualized freedom. As Tom Bunyard suggests in *Debord, Time and Spectacle*, overcoming the spectacle's imposition of "a state of separation from history itself" required us to abolish the barrier between art, labor, and life, to "realise art and poetry in lived time."[12] To break away from the spectacle, then, meant forging a different temporal arrangement, a different mode of existence no longer dominated by the fevered repetitive pace of commodity.

When enough people introduce a common rhythm counter to the intent of authoritarian space, it creates a different rubric of possibility. The economic, technological, and cultural forces that have alienated music, making it predictable and mitigating our experience of it, are reversed, even if only temporarily. As a collective, more rewarding temporality is reasserted *en masse*, the spatial confines on time show themselves to be pliable.

Each moment that this new, collective, temporal arrangement imposes becomes a moment of *jetztzeit*, not unlike the instances of psychedelic reason we see at the height of rave. If a mass, insurgent phenomenon like that scene presented the possibility to imagine urban space radically reorganized, then its subsequent (albeit short-lived) politicization, bringing it into conflict with forces that needed space commodified, was inevitable. The separation between carnival and demonstration collapses. Lenin's glib descriptor, "a festival of the oppressed," takes on new meaning.

This, in turn, is what makes moments such as those in Parliament Square in 2010 meaningful, and what makes such moments so terrifying to polite, bourgeois society. It is not merely that space or time are being redefined. It is that both could belong to those normally pushed out of its creation, experienced in a permanently

---

12 Tom Bunyard, *Debord, Time and Spectacle: Hegelian Marxism and Situationist Theory* (Leiden: Brill, 2018) p.363.

and radically different mode. Futures once abandoned are revived and implanted back into the very spaces that pushed them aside. The utopian impulse that is nurtured when creating or even just listening to music becomes a mass imperative.

...how I got to Ferguson

This relationship between space and time, between being and becoming, is also the key locus between music and protest. Even lyrical content takes a back seat to this relationship, for if the sonic dynamics of a song don't match the attempt to change the where and when, if they aren't actively defined toward that end by artist or protester, then even the most militant lyrics fall flat.

At its most essential, this spatio-temporal entanglement presents us with the conflict between music's ability to let us dream of life lived at a different pace – filled with a more enriched time – and the very real, very physical obstacles that the built world places on that future. Privatized listening – in the form of streaming services and personal mobile devices – buttresses this spatial domination of time through its ability to isolate the listener. Breaking music out of this alienated state, making it once again a common and democratic good, pulls at the limited shapes of daily life.

Thus we see, in some of the earliest days of the Black Lives Matter movement, a kind of conversation develop, a feedback loop between demonstrators seeking to transform their environment, the artists who see and hear a different mode of being in the demonstrators' actions, the attempts of these artists to relay this ruptural mode back into the world, and the attempt on the part of demonstrators to reinterpret these works in their swiftly changing context.

ANACHRONISM, ATTACK

During the initial two weeks of unrest in 2014 that followed the police killing of Black teenager Michael Brown in Ferguson, Missouri, numerous recording artists spoke in support of the protesters. No surprise that much of this support came from the hip-hop community. A few days into the uprising, the European tour of Los Angeles industrial rap group Clipping. was canceled at the last minute. The members – MC and lyricist Daveed Diggs (before his days in the hit Broadway musical *Hamilton*), and producers William Hutson and Jonathan Snipes (both veterans of LA's experimental noise scene) – met at the studio to record a new track.

The music of Clipping. had always been an experiment in harshness. An early review described the group's tracks as "from the club you wish you hadn't gone to." These were violent and unrelenting tracks, both lyrically and musically. Clipping.'s members had been open about the contradiction they explored, both taking a cue from and subverting rap's expectations and conventions. That day, they had Ferguson on their mind.

"Each of us had spent the previous several days following the news of protests in Ferguson, MO," wrote Hutson. "We couldn't bring ourselves to think about anything else, so we decided to direct our fear, our revulsion, our heartbreak into a new track."

The result was "Knees on the Ground," which Hutson called "a paradigmatic white-cop-kills-an-unarmed-black-kid-and-gets-away-with-it tale — a story that happens all the fucking time in the US." It is a disorienting song, but no more disorienting than the unmoored anxieties of systemic neglect. Or the rage that it strains to hold back.

By the time of the Ferguson uprising, the small city had become a textbook example of how America's cities were arranging and enclosing their surplus populations.

As with the rest of the rust belt, most decent-paying blue collar jobs had vanished from the area. Fifty years prior, Ferguson had been a comfortable, majority white and middle-class suburb. But wave after wave of disinvestment and job flight had turned the city into a kind of soft sacrifice zone. At the time of Mike Brown's murder, 67% of Ferguson residents were Black, with an official poverty rate twice the national average. In the wake of the protests, it became increasingly clear that the city's police department – like those in so many other cities – patrolled the poorest areas with the aim of serving residents with hefty fines that could provide revenue for the Ferguson city government.[13]

"If blues culture had developed under the conditions of oppressive, forced labor," wrote Jeff Chang in *Can't Stop, Wont' Stop*, "hip-hop culture would arise from the conditions of no work." In a world where there was industry to speak of in Ferguson, with a strong labor movement to accompany it, it would be easy to picture mass strikes as a component of the protests. But life in Ferguson had become too unpredictable, too tense, too arrhythmic – with the labor movement in too much of a state of demoralized confusion – for something like this to be possible. Clipping.'s 'Knees on the Ground' took this very literally. There is no distinctive beat to the song. Though Diggs' lyrics are delivered in an almost robotic cadence, the only percussive element is the sound of the cop's staccato pound on the front door. Until the chorus, that is, when all beats fall away, and there's nothing but the melancholy notes of finally drowning after a life of trying to swim against the tide.

---

13 Campbell Robertson, 'A City Where Policing, Discrimination and Raising Revenue Went Hand in Hand', *New York Times* (4 March 2015), https://www.nytimes.com/2015/03/05/us/us-details-a-persistent-pattern-of-police-discrimination-in-a-small-missouri-city.html.

> Times have made a choice of what to keep and what to throw away
>
> Everything ingrained comes to a point so sharp, could cut a piece a day
>
> And it bleeds on the ground, keep your knees on the ground, where they belong
>
> Keep your knees on the ground, where they belong

The chaos of experimental poet and noise artist Moor Mother's 'Creation Myth', the first track on her debut album *Fetish Bones*, takes this rhythmic unmooring to an even more extreme degree. Moor Mother – real name Camae Ayewa – is one half of the Black Quantum Futurism collective in Philadelphia, which, through art, literature, music, and organizing, seek to build an explicitly Afrofuturist political praxis. BQF rejects what it identifies as Eurocentric conceptions of space and time. Naturally, this methodology found itself into the composition of *Fetish Bones*.

"I studied every race riot that I could find," Ayewa told *Quietus*, "that was really the first part of writing the poem, doing all the research and reading and not just doing a Google search one day and feeling like I had all the information... The flow of history happens naturally; it was a lot to condense but the way that it just flows was quite interesting. It's a queer timeline that's just not linear, but some of the same kind of things are happening again, some of the things could as well be recent events."[14]

To say 'Creation Myth' has percussion is only to acknowledge that it assaults the listener with an irregular cacophony of thuds and screeches. It is the sound

---

[14] Elizabeth Aubrey, "Time Doesn't Feel Like a Linear Progression' – Moor Mother Interviewed', *Quietus* (17 April 2017), https://thequietus.com/articles/22207-moor-mother-interview.

of ordered time being ripped open, creating a rift in which all the ignored violence that haunts history comes barreling forward. Ferguson, in this harsh noise poem, is a culmination.

> I've been bleeding since 1866
> Dragged my bloody self to 1919
> And bled through the summer being slaughtered by whites
> A flux of chaos came after...
>
> And by the time I got to Watts
> I was missing most of my limbs
> Still had enough blood in my throat to gargle up nine words
> I resist to being both the survivor and victim...
>
> Some of us did just die while giving birth
> While protesting for the freedom of our sons
> And only God knows how I made it to Ferguson

Both 'Creation Myth' and 'Knees on the Ground' are remarkable examples of artists capturing the unmoored temporalities of racialized violence, psychic trauma, and an economics of systematic deprivation. Both attempt to reshape and make literal a long trajectory of disaster and the desperate attempt to break with it. In their case, it is the sound and feel of uprising bringing themselves into the minds and creative processes of artists, historical rupture meme-ing itself through rhythm. But as we've established, this relationship goes both directions: when protest itself reinterprets music.

'Hell You Talmbout' was quite obviously written to be used during a march. The only instrumentation is from a marching band drumline. Spearheaded by psychedelic soul artist Janelle Monáe and featuring members of their Wondaland Art Society, its lyrics are simple: the names of Black people killed by cops and racist vigilantes – Trayvon Martin, Aiyana Jones, Michael Brown, Eric Garner, Sandra Bland – with the demand that we "say their names." If it sounds like something that could be (and is!) chanted, then that's no accident.

An even starker example is in Kendrick Lamar's 'Alright', the fourth single from *To Pimp a Butterfly*. The track's video – featuring Lamar carried in a car by police officers and dancing on top of light poles before being shot down by a cop – makes clear enough that Lamar had police violence and Black resilience in mind. What seems to have solidified the connection, however, was the response of Movement for Black Lives organizers to the police at their conference at Cleveland State University in July of 2015.

When transit authority police near campus arrested a Black 14-year-old allegedly for intoxication on a bus, M4BL members surrounded the cruiser he was locked in. Police responded with pepper spray. Protesters didn't move. Instead, they started chanting the chorus of Kendrick Lamar's track: "We gon' be alright! We gon' be alright!" A city street which otherwise would have quickly been returned to its pace of humdrum regularity, was instead brought to a halt. The heavy-handed policing normally integrated into the motions of everyday life was surrounded and singled out as an obstacle to a decent future by those most at risk.

This is where, finally, we see music's utopian impulse redeemed and valorized. Its rhythm, its potential signification of ordinary people in control of time, is seized upon collectively, reinterpreted from the bottom up, weaponized against a prevailing order of social death.

Part Four
Revolt Against Exterminism

> "Humankind, which in Homer's time was an object of contemplation for the Olympian gods, now is one for itself. Its self-alienation has reached such a degree that it can experience its own destruction as an aesthetic pleasure of the first order. This is the situation of politics which Fascism is rendering aesthetic. Communism responds by politicizing art."
> Walter Benjamin, 'The Work of Art in the Age of Mechanical Reproduction'

> "As long as space and time divide you from anyone you love… love will simply have no choice but to go into battle with space and time and, furthermore, to win."
> James Baldwin

Singing in dark times

March, 2020. The world had already been warned of coronavirus. We saw it coming. But with most governments either unprepared or criminally indifferent, we could do little but watch it spread. Now it was at the front door of everyone who had one. Some countries locked down quicker than others, but all eventually locked down.

Apocalypse, spoken about in increasingly dramatic tones by climate scientists, suddenly felt very real. Our psychological cognizance was catching up to reality. Photos of mass graves on New York's Hart Island landed on our screens. Then came the attempts to assuage panic. In fact, there had been a potter's field cemetery at Hart Island since the 1860s, with over a million corpses buried there. Implied but unanswered was what kind of society it is that needs to maintain anonymous mass graves.

Pictures out of Italy were equally terrifying. To many, the country appeared paralyzed as it sunk into the depths of a new plague. News spread of people isolated in their homes with the bodies of dead family members for days on end. So did pictures of army truck convoys, carrying untold numbers of dead.

So, thankfully, did videos of Italians with a modicum of hope. Sometimes they were lone voices, sometimes they were part of a group, and occasionally they had musical accompaniment. One song seemed to catch particular attention as it wafted down the empty streets of Rome: "Bella Ciao."

Long before its use in the popular Spanish crime show *La Casa de Papel* made it globally recognizable, "Bella Ciao" had a history. Like so many folk songs, its authors are unknown, its current form emerged out of decades of evolution, verses and tunes added over the course of years by this or that anonymous singer. According to Jerry Silverman in *Songs that Made History Around the World*, the song's earliest versions can be traced to women working in the rice paddies of Italy's Po Valley in the late nineteenth century. Its original lyrics bristled against back-breaking work, low pay, and overzealous managers.[1]

In the 1940s, during the final days of Mussolini's fascist regime, the lyrics were repurposed to tell the stories of the anti-fascist partisans. To this day, in some corners of polite Italian society, singing "Bella Ciao" is still seen as rude or insulting. Which says something about the parts of the country's history that they would rather not talk about, and what made it a rallying point for the Italian New Left. Indeed, "Bella Ciao," as it was sung across the empty streets of Rome, sounded like something haunting, something which should be dead but is not. Its tones are at once melancholy and defiant, insisting on beauty even in the face of death.

> E se io muoio da partigiano
> O bella ciao, bella ciao, bella ciao, ciao, ciao
> E se io muoio da partigiano
> Tu mi devi seppellir
>
> E seppellire lassù in montagna
> O bella ciao, bella ciao, bella ciao, ciao, ciao
> E seppellire lassù in montagna
> Sotto l'ombra di un bel for
> ...
> And if I die a partisan
> O bella ciao, bella ciao, bella ciao, ciao, ciao
> And if I die a partisan
> You will have to bury me
>
> So bury me then, upon the mountain
> O bella ciao, bella ciao, bella ciao, ciao, ciao
> So bury me then, upon the mountain
> In the shade of a bright flower

---

[1] Jerry Silverman, *Songs That Made History Around the World* (Fenton: Mel Bay Publications, 2011) p.43.

The invocation of a storied anti-fascist folk song during a plague has turned out to be fitting. It's clear by now how badly the world's governments have botched this pandemic. The scenes of predominantly middle-class and white anti-lockdown protests – literally calling for working-class people to be sacrificed so the well-to-do can have their country clubs back – were terrifying enough. Even more terrifying was how little resistance they encountered. Far from it, these actions had sympathetic audiences in the halls of power, including the highest offices. Donald Trump, Rodrigo Duterte, Narendra Modi, Jair Bolsonaro, Viktor Orban. Liberal and centrist opposition has only occasionally gone beyond rhetoric. Most of the time it has failed to be an opposition at all, instead seeking compromise or accommodation.

It is still shocking to many of us that this kind of barbarism is not just tolerated but embraced. Capital has long been adept at masking its death drive. Now it no longer needs the mask, not that it ever covered much in the first place. The terrifying inhuman moments of recent years – the disdain for human dignity and basic democratic norms, the open applause for violence and death – these are simply capitalism baring its teeth a little bit more.

In 1980, EP Thompson coined the term "exterminism." The veteran Marxist theorist was at that time heavily active in the Campaign for Nuclear Disarmament. For him, the atomic annihilation of Hiroshima and Nagasaki by American forces in 1945 was "the first annunciation of exterminist technology."[2] Exterminism, as the term implies, is the willingness of a system to dispose of its surplus populations, to lay waste to large swathes of the planet,

2 E.P. Thompson, 'Notes on Exterminism, the Last Stage of Civilization', *New Left Review*, no. 121 (May/June 1980), https://www.versobooks.com/blogs/3022-notes-on-exterminism-the-last-stage-of-civilization.

turning whole regions into sacrifice zones. In Thompson's view, the domination of human beings by clock time, which he had identified in "Time, Work-Discipline and Capital," now bent in the direction of oblivion.

The year 1945 should loom large for us too. Many climate scientists see it as the inaugural year of the Anthropocene. It tracks. Any system willing to split the atom for the sake of mass destruction is easily able to undo the balance of global ecology for the sake of economic growth. The widening of the metabolic rift that has given rise to increasingly erratic weather patterns, floods, hurricanes, droughts, is also what has allowed the coronavirus to jump into the human population.

Just like the consequences of climate change, the consequences of the new plague are disproportionately borne by the anachronized, those pushed aside from the full range of resources: workers, the poor, people of color, undocumented immigrants, the disabled and immunocompromised, those outside the conservative norms of sex and gender. And the forces that are most eager to throw these populations on the sacrifice block – be they political leaders or on-the-ground shock troops – are willing to be the foot soldiers of this impulse, to bring it from idea into reality.

In this sense, exterminism is not particularly reliant on nuclear weapons, climate change, or plagues, but the balance of social forces. It is, in Thompson's words, "characteristics of a society – expressed, in differing degrees, within its economy, its polity, and its ideology – which thrust it in a direction whose outcome must be the extermination of multitudes."[3]

Exterminism and fascism are intertwined. The mass psychological impulse toward the former is organized and weaponized into its ultimate political form

---

[3] ibid.

in the latter. But the impulse is always there, inherent in the DNAs of capitalism and empire, its essence potentized by every conquered region and every minute lorded over the powerless. Aimé Césaire, in *Discourse on Colonialism*, writes what is done to the marginal and anachronized must eventually be turned inward against even the most seemingly secure worker:

> People are surprised, they become indignant. They say: "How strange! But never mind – it's Nazism, it will pass!" And they wait, and they hope; and they hide the truth from themselves, that it is barbarism, the supreme barbarism, the crowning barbarism that sums up the daily barbarisms; that it is Nazism, yes, but that before they were its victims, they were its accomplices; that they tolerated that Nazism before it was inflicted on them, that they absolved it, shut their eyes to it, legitimized it, because, until then, it had been applied only to non-European peoples; that they have cultivated that Nazism, that they are responsible for it, and that before engulfing the whole edifice of Western, Christian civilization in its reddened waters, it oozes, seeps and trickles from every crack.[4]

This is not to say that all working and poor people are now forced to deal with the same levels of systematic violence as the immigrant worker, the queer worker, or workers of color. Merely that on a long enough timeline, every working-class life is disposable.

Once again, we are forced to face the reality of this barbarism. Whether it finds expression in fascism or a more prosaic authoritarianism, it is part of

---

4 Aimé Cesaire, *Discourse On Colonialism* [1955], trans. by Joan Pinkham (New York: Monthly Review Press, 2000) p.36.

our political landscape. So are its cultures of cruelty and atomization, its geographies of death, its temporalities of despair.

Sinking ships

It was a month after the election of Donald Trump in the United States. The news was of a fire in Oakland, California, at an artists' residence and performance-exhibition space known as the Ghost Ship. On the night of the fire, independent house music label 100% Silk had hosted a party there. When the flames had finally been doused, 36 people were dead. Most of them were artists or musicians, some students. Many were queer or trans. Many were people of color.

Some of the artists had a profile. Cash Askew, 22 years old at the time of her death, was one half of the dark dream pop band Them Are Us Too, who had signed to independent label Dais Records in 2014 and toured nationally. Joey Casio, ex-boyfriend of Bikini Kill drummer Tobi Vail, was a big influence in the collision between electro and punk.

A specific confluence of factors had to come together for something like the Ghost Ship disaster to be possible. The first is gentrification. As had happened in Detroit and many other deindustrializing cities, the disused warehouses and industrial spaces of the Bay Area had been transformed into cheap residential and studio space. This was partly out of necessity, a reflection of the United States' anemic public funding for the arts. Still, it did the trick. That is, until the bohemian-chic warehouse loft became trendy and the bourgeois wanted the city centers back. Their well-moneyed demands were met, as we know, through rising rents, overdevelopment, and increased policing.

This had the effect of turning those few warehouse arts communes still in existence into death traps, as well as opportunities for the dangerously dishonest. The Ghost Ship had roughly twenty residents, all artists who lived and worked there. There was no working sprinkler system. Fire extinguishers were few. And the "master tenant" at the Ghost Ship was known for unscrupulous behavior. But the fact that he only charged $300 to $600 a month for rent, in a city where the average one-bedroom cost over $2000, earned him few complaints.

"Residents of these 'live-work' artistic communes often live in fear of losing these spaces," reported *Rolling Stone* magazine in the days after the fire, "further keeping them from reporting unsafe living conditions to the city which could potentially shut down the space if not up to code."[5]

Even as local arts and music scenes mourned, a newly emboldened far-right saw opportunity. Neo-fascist online communities started to see messages like the following posted:

> These places are open hotbeds of liberal radicalism and degeneracy and now YOU can stop them by reporting all such places you may be or may become aware of to the authorities, specifically the local fire marshel [sic].
>
> Watch them and follow them to their hives. Infiltrate social circles, go to parties/events, record evidence, and report it. We've got them on the run but now we must crush their nests before they can regroup!

---

5 'Inside Oakland Ghost Ship Warehouse Before the Fire', *Rolling Stone* (5 December 2016), https://www.rollingstone.com/music/music-lists/inside-oakland-ghost-ship-warehouse-before-the-fire-109288/messy-collection-109883/.

> MAGA [Make America Great Again] my brothers and happy hunting!

It was mostly an empty threat, but it also reflected the war-like spatial politics of fascism. Confident fascists are always engaged in a turf war. They are always looking for the next space, not so much to govern as to grasp, squeeze, and force in line. All dissident or unpredictable denizens will either comply – where to go, when to go there, how to be – or be eliminated from that space. If that means these spaces are transformed into charred wastelands, so be it.

Though nothing concrete came of these specific threats to shut down independent arts spaces, we do see this same imperative in the actions of the American far-right in the months and years following. Whether it was in Charlottesville, Long Beach, or the state capitol buildings of Michigan, Florida, California, even the houses of congress, this is a movement that requires spatial domination. And, whether its devotees know it or not, it is a movement operating on fertile ground, provided by the same liberal order it disdains.

In *Four Futures*, using Thompson's framework, Peter Frase sees the seeds of exterminism gestating in the neoliberal geographies of the privileged: the gated community, the fortressed penthouse, the $3 million luxury bunker – complete with swimming pools and a wine bar – now being constructed by the very wealthy. Many of whom see themselves as tolerant, inclusive, voting center-left so long as taxes aren't raised. None of this makes their space less deadly or oppressive.[6]

Frase calls these spaces "inverted gulags," designed not to keep the undesirables confined but rather to exile them to a dying planet and dwindling resources. These

---

6 Peter Frase, *Four Futures: Life After Capitalism* (London: Verso Books, 2016).

spaces are already somewhat sheltered from the current, slow-motion apocalypse. Come the cataclysm, whatever form it may take, the more deliberately designed and airtight will be the floating islands of leisure, blissfully unaware of the disasters outside. Inside, history never happened, and never needed to end. It is an increasingly attractive existence to the wealthy and powerful. With the rise of what we now refer to as "eco-fascism," dedicated to hoarding resources for those deemed most deserving, the inverted gulag has found its foot soldiers.

Digital diktat

Once again, as physical spaces for creative expression are squeezed into non-existence, the virtual spaces – privately owned, tightly controlled, perfectly tailored toward the capture and financialization of desire – step into their place. The outcome, a perverse syncopation with the arrhythmia of the authoritarian city, achieves what many attempts at direct repression cannot: consent to exploitation.

We should think, urgently, yet again, of Walter Benjamin, this time his 'The Work of Art in the Age of Mechanical Reproduction.' Here, Benjamin observes the way in which fascism rhythmically organizes masses of people against their own freedom. Describing the huge rallies that would see the movements of men, women, and children synchronized into the loving arms of an all-powerful fuehrer, Benjamin sees their creative urges diverted not into reshaping the world but into the illusion that someone else might reshape it for them. This is the aestheticization of politics. "The masses have a right to change property relations," Benjamin writes, "fascism seeks to give them an expression while preserving property."[7]

The algorithm, generating profit by isolating the consumer-user, creating and satisfying meaningless desires in the same motion, is perfectly suited for this. It would be hyperbolic to broadly paint the algorithm as innately fascist. Nonetheless, just as neoliberalism's austerian attacks have chipped away at social coherence consistently enough for fascism to find an opening, so is it easy to for the far-right to exploit our existence in the lonely network.

One can see and hear this clearly enough in what happened within a genre like vaporwave as the Trump years began. In the late aughts and early 2010s, vaporwave carried with it an unmistakable irony whose bite was broadly directed against late capitalist consumer culture. It also flourished primarily in virtual communities and message boards. If the online commons had ended up one big mall, then the crop of artists who pioneered the sound and aesthetic – Oneohtrix Point Never, James Ferraro, Vektroid and the many other aliases of Ramona Xavier – leaned into this truism until it popped at the seams.

Its emergence from experimental electronic subgenres like hypnagogic pop and chillwave already established a certain, quasi-psychedelic mandate. Its incorporation and reworking of highly artificial sounds and genres – synthesized smooth jazz, 90s computer ephemera, 80s video game soundtracks, hyper-neon glitch-art, and yes, muzak – were distorted and bent into each other. Its best compositions satirize a world of full-spectrum commodification and historical impasse. Even the genre's name, vaporwave, conjures up the notion of deflected futures haunting,

---

[7] Walter Benjamin, 'The Work of Art in the Age of Mechanical Reproduction,' (1936), https://www.marxists.org/reference/subject/philosophy/works/ge/benjamin.htm.

"vaporware" being the term for a promised tech product that never makes it to market.

"These artists," writes Grafton Tanner in *Babbling Corpse*, "are skeptical of capitalism's promise to redeem us in the name of material goods and of the nostalgia that hangs over an era obsessed with the clichés of history."[8] In other words, within the synthetic, there is a shadowed desire for the real, within the sounds of the past an alternative path that, with the right arrangement, becomes shockingly apparent.

Not long after Trump's election, a curious offshoot emerged. Fashwave: vaporwave for fascists. Its artists have names like Xurious and the ever-original Cyber Nazi. They produce songs like "Galactic Lebensraum," "Team White," and "Death to Traitors," layering swastikas and stock footage of fascist marches into their videos. Having already existed for a few years in the darker corners of the internet, Trump's election provided an opening to reach a larger audience.

Sound-wise, not much separates these songs from their non-fascist counterparts. Except for one ingredient: irony. There is far less of it in fashwave. Or at least it is deployed in a very different way. Much how the contemporary fascist leans into the utterly absurd level of violence inherent in their politics, so fashwave artist wink-and-nudge their audience, legitimizing themselves by provoking outrage in the flattened world of online discourse. Penn Bullock and Eli Perry write that fashwave

> ...exploits a vulnerability in vaporwave: its ambivalence about the cultural detritus that inspired it. This careful tension between irony and earnestness was part of what made vaporwave fun – it flirted with the implicit

---
8 Grafton Tanner, *Babbling Corpse: Vaporwave and the Commodification of Ghosts* (Alresford: Zero Books, 2016) p.xi.

transgressiveness of appreciating its aggressively commercial source material. But that ambiguity left the aesthetic distressingly easy for the alt-right to appropriate by stripping it of irony and playfulness – by taking it literally, as a glorification of capitalism... A glance at the album art of Cyber Nazi – with its jackbooted cyborg cops going door to door – shows how for fascists, this dystopia is utopia. Extrapolating from the 80s, fashwave embraces that decade's grim sci-fi forecasts as paradise.[9]

For a short time, some argued that the algorithms of YouTube naturally skewed in the direction of the alt-right, exposing viewers to more and more extreme content. While the veracity of this assertion is still being debated, the dehumanization required by fascism is aided by the depersonalization of the internet.

The privatization of cultural experience places the subject on a lone temporal fragment, drifting through an overwhelming and unstable moment in history. The denizen of the lonely crowd is more susceptible to the predations of fascist art precisely because it is similarly divorced from context. In this depersonalized milieu, irony falls flat, and bad faith runs rampant. Hence fashwave's ability to reach an audience far larger than the subculture's tiny numbers would otherwise be able to find.

The atomized consumer hears and sees themself the hero of a readymade fiction. The delusion of ultimate control – through conspiracy theory, for example – is easily able to step into the void left by a shrinking and

---

[9] Penn Bullock and Eli Perry, 'Trumpwave and Fashwave Are Just the Latest Disturbing Examples of the Far-Right Appropriating Electronic Music', *Noisey* (30 January 2017), https://www.vice.com/en/article/mgwk7b/fashwave-trumpwave-far-right-appropriating-electronic-music.

inaccessible social life. They are easily pulled into a telos of domination over the weak and unwanted.

It's why, even as fashwave artists were banned from YouTube and Spotify, the appeal of their poisonous worldview did not dissemble or dim among the converted. Rather, they retreated to new online communities and platforms, their own pods shielded from the consequence and causality of the rest of the world. While the mainstream, tolerant internet pushes the problem out of sight and mind, the problem has in fact worsened. More committed and more organized, it waits for the inevitable opportunity to reemerge. In the age of "platform capitalism," de-platforming changes very little.

Infrastructures of creative dissent

If there is any lesson in the evolution of fashwave out of vaporwave, it is that a liberatory subculture – to say nothing of counterculture – cannot thrive solely online. Any attempt to push back against the algorithm on its own terms proves futile. In early 2022, several high-profile recording artists announced that they were pulling their music from Spotify in protest of its inclusion and promotion of *The Joe Rogan Experience*. Rogan, one of the most obnoxiously Neanderthalic of today's "edgelord" podcasters, has long flirted with alt-right ideas, including Covid denialism and vaccine skepticism. Rogan is the most popular podcaster on Spotify, and one of the most hated.

First, Neil Young pulled his music. Then Joni Mitchell. Not long after that came India.Arie, who pointed to Rogan's own long history of racism. A handful of other artists followed suit, drawing a connection between Rogan and Spotify's refusal to pay artists more than a pittance. As of writing, these artists are still boycotting

Spotify. Rogan remains.

Motivations are one thing. Effectiveness is another. Online is enemy territory, meaning that it can be easily retooled to soften the blow of any boycott, lessening its impact, and metabolizing the protest into the rest of the flotsam already vying for your attention onscreen. It is not impossible for a boycott of Spotify or other streaming services to be successful. But it would need to root itself in where people exist, which, for the time being anyway, is still the physical, offline world.

This task relates to what Marxist sociologist Alan Sears calls "infrastructures of dissent." These infrastructures are, at their most basic, the groups and collective relationships that illustrate and mobilize common demands both within a specific community and across its borders, through cities and differently exploited groups. Across geographic separation and psychological atomization, these infrastructures are the atomic unit of practical solidarity.

In March of 2021, the newly-formed Union of Musicians and Allied Workers held rallies outside Spotify's offices in Los Angeles, New York, San Francisco, Boston, and other cities across the United States. This was part of the new union's "Justice at Spotify" campaign, which has demanded more equitable compensation for artists – a whopping penny per play – among other improvements. Most protests were on the smaller side, no more than a hundred people or so. Even so, the notion that composing, recording, and releasing music might be a form of labor (and therefore worthy of decent compensation) was enough to put Spotify on edge.

UMAW came together as venues all over the world shut down due to coronavirus. With so much of musicians' income reliant on what they earn at live performances, many found a huge chunk of their livelihoods vanished. Streaming services' criminally paltry payment structures became even more egregious.

Joshua Sushman, a multi-instrumentalist and UMAW member born and raised in Los Angeles, called what the streamer does the "muzak-ification" of music. "The goal of Spotify is to reframe how music is listened to," they said. "They're trying to prioritize the playlist, right? They connect to the playlist because that's how they commodify music more easily. You just put it on in the background."[10]

Says Sushman, this undercuts artists' freedom to push boundaries and expectations, and in turn for people to discover music that might provoke them to look at the world in a different way. "I don't think people create relationships with Spotify's playlist," they continued. "It's actually an impossibility, because it's a naturally ephemeral thing."

That's not to say Spotify is the union's only target. Rather, it is an avatar for everything wrong in an exploitative music industry. To Sushman, there is a direct connection between this process, the cheapening and narrowing of music's scope, and the gentrification of cities. "It's harder to live here," they said. "So the access to space that we used to have is dwindling. And when we have less space, it's harder to make music."[11]

This is particularly evident at Spotify's Los Angeles headquarters. Forty years prior, the emptying warehouses of what would become LA's Arts District were, like in the Bay Area and elsewhere, inhabited by artists and musicians in search of cheap space. Independent coffee shops, galleries, and music venues sprung up, providing

---

10 Alexander Billet, 'A New Union of Musicians is Taking On Spotify', *Jacobin* (12 April 2021), https://jacobin.com/2021/04/union-musicians-allied-workers-spotify-streaming.
11 ibid.

time and space for bands like The Fall and Sonic Youth. Today, with a few dwindling exceptions, these buildings house industry "disruptors" like WeWork, Honey, and Soylent. Rents, residential and commercial, are prohibitively expensive. Spotify's office is, oddly, invisible from the street, tucked away in a courtyard off the corner of Mateo and Palmetto.

Though the demonstration was small, it was also loud. Protesters beat out rhythms on drums and blew trumpets. It was a short march from the street corner through the courtyard to Spotify's offices. Predictably, the Los Angeles Police Department showed up, reminding the crowd that they were on private property, and they would be arrested if they didn't leave. Spotify's offices were locked; those inside were unwilling to receive UMAW's demands. Union member Julia Holter duct-taped them next to the doors.

It is difficult to imagine anyone at these relatively small demonstrations was expecting to push through, to occupy Spotify's offices and demand it address its undemocratic distribution model. One day, perhaps. In the meantime, these actions play a role in deciding how to create art and organization.

For Josephine Shetty, a musician and singer who records and performs under the moniker Kohinoorgasm, UMAW's vision must be ambitious if it is to succeed. "We are subject to a power imbalance, not just as musicians," she says. "A big project of UMAW is to include all music workers: venue workers, label workers, the person who works the door, the person who sells the merch, everybody who's involved in this industry."[12]

At the time of the day of action, UMAW was in the

---

12 Josephine Shetty, 'Musicians Need to Organize Collectively, as Workers', *Jacobin* (16 January 2021), https://jacobin.com/2021/01/musicians-workers-collective-organizing.

process of forming locals. It was also setting up working groups to hash out ways to effectively relate to other movements: Black Lives Matter, Green New Deal, abolition of prisons and racist immigration enforcement. Among union members, there is a clear sense that the conditions under which they are free to make music are connected to making the world a freer place more generally. Discovering and strengthening these links is both urgent and cannot be rushed. They must be thrashed out over the process of collective discussion and experiment. Between the starting point and the vision, the construction of an infrastructure of creative dissent proves essential.

This kind of work is painstaking, often yielding nothing perceivable for years. And while it would be simplistic to draw so straight a line between these efforts and the explosive moments that draw hundreds of thousands or even millions onto the streets, there is no denying that the ability to sustain these movements is in large part down to the prior strength of these infrastructures.

Abolition and creativity

The year before the pandemic saw the stirrings of what, if not for the intervention of a deadly virus, might have become a new wave of global protest: Hong Kong, Lebanon, Chile, Haiti, South Africa, Catalonia, Sudan, France. Some included brilliant and creative incorporations of music into a public sphere brought to the brink of transformation.

In Haiti, demonstrations against the corrupt presidency of Jovenel Moïse reappropriated the rabòday song "Jojo Domi Deyo" – already highly popular at Carnival time – into a song of mockery and derision. In Lebanon, the massive protests against inequality, government-stoked sectarianism, and a skyrocketing cost of living were likened by some commentators to "a rave." One local DJ, based in Tripoli, set up his sound system on a balcony to turn the streets below into a dance floor.

In the United States, the uprising would come only several months into the pandemic, after most of us had spent months either crammed in our homes or forced to work in dangerous conditions, wondering what the world would look like after it was over. In this respect, the militant demonstrations and urban rebellions in the weeks after the police murder of George Floyd were an outpouring against a pervading culture of death in which racism is a leading edge. Donald Trump's blustering, bellicose response during the uprising's height – threatening to send in the military, encouragement of racist vigilantes – hit home that these were the stakes. So, for that matter, did the heavy-handed tactics on the part of police: kettling of protesters, the use of rubber bullets and tear gas, driving cruisers through crowds.

These demonstrations were certainly large, often drawing tens of thousands into the streets at short notice. Many of them also displayed an unmistakable spirit of mutual aid. Activist groups distributed masks, water, even saline solution for use in case of tear gas. Finally, though far more spontaneous and less organized, protesters' rage often spilled over into an instinctive urge to reshape the city. Media's reference to these acts as mindless vandalism obscured the strong symbolism at play.

Yes, there was graffiti. Most often, it was graffiti demanding we remember the names of George Floyd, Breonna Taylor, and other victims of racist and police violence. Yes, shop windows were smashed, often to have their contents lifted. Most often it was from the kind of unwieldy big box stores that served to homogenize neighborhoods, displacing poor and working-class residents while also dangling in front of them goods they could not afford.

In short, this vandalism and looting was as creative as it was destructive. At some demonstrations, plywood used to board up shops was turned into murals with portraits and quotes from Angela Davis, Malcolm X, or James Baldwin. It was not uncommon in many of the larger mobilizations to see trucks outfitted with sound systems, even live bands, DJs and MCs. Some demonstrators drove their cars alongside marchers, careful to go a slow pace, their friends sitting out of windows and sunroofs with signs, stereos blasting.

This was exactly what John Berger pointed to when he wrote of the nature of mass demonstrations. It is also an echo of the situationists' ideas of how mass rebellion punctures the predictability of time.[13] Considering the frequency with which Black and Latino youth are hassled or threatened for the volume of their music, the stories of Michael Stewart, Israel Hernández-Llach and other graffiti artists killed by police officers, one has to acknowledge the sheer bravery in these destructive-creative expressions. These are, in the formulation of David Harvey, moments when, in reshaping ourselves, we also reshape the city.

And there were indeed instances in which the city was literally reshaped. By the end of the first week, the station of Minneapolis' Third Police Precinct had been burned to the ground. In Seattle, police abandoned the East Precinct to protesters, who took over the building

---

[13] The situationists had a history of unconditionally supporting urban rebellions, not just in Europe but in the United States, too, particularly in relation to police racism. As Frances Stracey chronicles in her book *Constructed Situations*, the Situationist International published full-throated support for the Los Angeles Watts uprising in 1965, describing Black residents' attacks on police and large businesses as a particularly direct form of community decommodification.

and surrounding blocks, transforming them into what was alternately called the Capitol Hill Autonomous Zone or the Capitol Hill Organized Protest. Activists, organizers and artists congregated at the CHAZ/CHOP, arguing strategy and planning actions, often organizing education and entertainment too.

This desire to reshape also ran through the policy demands that came out of Black Lives Matter in 2020. They were obviously desires to abolish. But as the best abolitionists remind us, to abolish means as much to build as it does to tear down. It is not just that police must be defunded, nor just that these funds be redirected to schools, housing, or healthcare. Every structure we rely on must be revamped wholesale.

In the United States, public assistance programs – including healthcare and housing – are often interwoven with work requirements, monitoring a recipient's job searches, and arbitrary suspension of benefits. This increasing level of restriction matches the deep cuts these programs have been subjected to; as more rules are put in place, the excuses to deprive the poor with a basic standard of living flourish. As public schools have been progressively defunded, curricula slashed and classrooms overcrowded, they have strengthened their relationships with police. Some cities have established separate police departments whose only purview is the patrol of the public school system.

In *A World Without Police*, Geo Maher writes of how the reemergence of Black Lives Matter allowed for this creative-destructive ethos to gain a foothold.

> The George Floyd rebellions sparked nationwide calls to defund the police, and for many, this naturally means redirecting those funds toward social workers, mental health

professionals, and schools. As we have seen, however, each of these institutions is increasingly complicit in the broader carceral system, functioning more like the police and handing more people over to prisons every day. As a result, abolitionists today remind us that we must also *reimagine* welfare institutions as part of a broader abolitionist project. [14]

Radically remaking these institutions – decoupling them from austerity and the carceral state – should be the brass tacks of any socialist project. It may be difficult at first to clearly see how art and music fit into such a project. But approaching these structures of daily life with the full spirit of the radical imagination, we glean two conclusions.

First, there is a direct link between infrastructures of dissent and the transformation of the institutions of daily life. The radical democracy needed to build the former fully and effectively is also the starting point for the latter. We might then say that the infrastructure of dissent is the seed of the transformed institution.

Second, there is a pedagogical element to art and music. Thinking back to the example of the Chicago Teachers Union, we remember that the arts, and their attendant nurture of imagination, are essential for basic intellectual and emotional development in young students, as well as fomenting a sense of teamwork, empathy, and mutual interest. This pedagogy does not end after the student reaches adulthood. In the case of music, it is the assertion of control over time – both collective and individual – that is most salient.

For time inevitably becomes history, and if time under capitalism is the repetitive, empty time of

---

14 Geo Maher, *A World Without Police* (London: Verso, 2021). p.158.

commodity, then history will also inevitably belong to commodity. Dis-alienating and democratizing life, therefore, requires a kind of leap into the tightly wound rhythms of modernity, with their tightrope-like precarity, and exploding them, demystifying them, turning time itself into something that can be wielded rather than something that controls us.

The double-edged nature of popular music places it on this tightrope. It also begs for a push, to collide with the rest of the world in such a way that the arrhythmia of modern urban life is brought to heel. As Mark Abel writes:

> Groove, in its best manifestations, bears within itself an aesthetic critique of the alienated temporality of contemporary capitalism, and figures a demand for the collective control of time and history in which the time of the universe and the time of humanity would finally be reconciled.[15]

Constructing this mode of existence, finding new ways to experience it, should be one of the aims of radical organization. It need not always be done through music or art, but by that same token there is no reason to refuse their avenues of learning and self-discovery. When we are grabbed my music, we briefly feel what it is to be in equilibrium – harmony, if you will – with ourselves and each other. Such a radical democratic mandate, therefore, requires us to seek out, as the situationists insisted, ways we might "realise art and poetry in lived time."

The future, uncancelled

Perceptive readers will have noticed a kind of musical evolutionary chronology on the pages of *Shake the*

[15] Abel, *Groove*, pp.255-256.

City. In attempting to find examples of music that pushes against the spatial boundaries of capital and empire, a rough lineage of style has emerged. Call it an alternative ontology of the sound system. From blues and jazz into rock and R&B, which then found itself repurposed into the beginnings of reggae, then reggae into dub, dub to hip-hop, but also into house, techno and rave, the sounds of which are then pushed into the damp isolations of dubstep, even as grime manically digs its way out from under the wreckage and vaporwave oozes through its cracks.

Like any genealogy, it is bound to be incomplete. Nevertheless, it is a genealogy, and reveals a throughline in the social-creative process. Just as each genre reaches the limits of its aesthetic, there are inevitably artists willing to keep pushing. Technologies, sounds, and gestures calcified into staid conventions come to be used in a way that bucks predictability. The difference may have been in the sound itself, a new context, or simply that the sound had not reached so many ears yet.

In all of these, rupture is portended. The blue note wriggles its way off the fretboard, the record scratch becomes a way for hip-hop to communicate tension and excitement. Noise becomes music, and lonely songs on barren streets are sung by larger and larger throngs of people. Empty time is interrupted. The airtight glass of music-as-commodity is shattered. *Jetztzeit*. For that short time, the past is shown to be unfinished, and those abandoned to it are unexpectedly now at the vanguard of events.

This is the essence of experimentation. It is necessarily utopian: seeing the world as it is, asking what if it worked differently, investigating ways it might be so. It is also central to what Franco "Bifo" Berardi calls "futurability," the ability to make thinkable a future worthy of the name, and with it a human subject emancipated from the logics of capital. Bifo describes a landscape at home in the formulations of capitalist realism, of the cultural-technological configurations that fragment the social valence of music and engender a state of arrhythmia. "The hyper-stimulated body is simultaneously alone and hyper-connected," he writes, "the cooperating brains have no collective body and the private bodies have no collective brain."[16]

To Bifo, breaking ourselves out of the futurelessness of empire, desiccated democracy, and late neoliberal capitalism, requires building new connections of compassion and solidarity. The molecular pedagogies of art and music, their ability to embed the experience of empathy, shared destiny and common temporality, become essential here. They help us map connections between otherwise disparate internal lives. The adage of art "expanding horizons," then, is not just rhetoric. Because eventually, inevitably, regardless of whether or not we are the ones defining its limits, imagined horizons become literal.

Contrasted with the false empowerment offered by the fascist aestheticization of violence and domination, a radical and liberatory employment of music allows for its organic politicization. It allows us to feel that full control over one's time and space – the most fundamental elements of existence – can only be exercised collectively and from the bottom-up.

New songs, new again

The history that hangs over the Plaza Bernardo Leighton in Santiago is an ambivalent one. Named for Chile's centrist senator and former secretary of labor who was left brain-damaged by an assassination attempt from General Augusto Pinochet's military junta, the wide-open city square culminates in the Basílica de los

---

16 Franco "Bifo" Berardi, *Futurability: The Age of Impotence and the Horizon of Possibility* (London: Verso, 2019) pp.50-51.

Sacramentinos. As with many other Catholic basilicas, its steeples draw the eye upward and into the skies. Once again, the built world is one that hovers above our repetitive, consequence-bound lives. On this particular day, it was the motions in the square itself, the kinetic energy of performance melting into a utopian refusal, that defined it. When history converges on a point in time by its own accord.

Thousands of people occupy a town square, 500 of whom are either orchestra or choir. The synchronized movement of string instruments and bows is clear, so are the motions of the orchestra's conductor. The tune is defiant, asserting that while it has been sung before and will likely be sung again, this time strives to be different. As its chorus starts, the singing gives way to chanting. "El pueblo, unido, jamas sera vencido!" The chanting continues, grows louder, and the division between orchestra and audience breaks down.

It is October of 2019, and the people of Chile have brought the country to a standstill. What started out a few weeks before as a refusal to pay increased public transport prices has generalized into a broad rebellion against profound inequality and a lack of basic democracy that has persisted long after the military junta's end.

Pinochet's notoriously murderous seventeen-year tenure as Chile's president has become a bloody symbol for the brutality of anti-communism in Latin America and around the world. Overthrowing the democratic socialist experiment of leftist president Salvador Allende in 1973, it massacred thousands of leftists, trade unionists, and indigenous activists to cling to power. This was a regime that could plausibly be called fascist, and was most certainly exterminist in its approach to the marginalized and oppressed. It even banned indigenous musical instruments, such as the *charango*.

Pinochet's government enshrined the free market into Chile's constitution. Neoliberal orthodoxy, the wholesale retooling of the state for private accumulation of profit at the expense of the needs of the people – from privatized healthcare to education fees, from bans on rent control to limits on labor organization – was entrenched in the country. Even after Pinochet stepped down and Chile reverted to a nominal state of democracy, that constitution endured.

Hence the "social explosion," or *Estadillo Social* as it came to be known in Chile. Residents ransack and burn massive chain stores. Students occupy campuses. Demonstrators defy the orders of police and army by the thousands. Later, Chilean police will be found to have employed especially brutal tactics in attempting to subdue the protests, including torture and aiming rubber bullets at protesters' faces. Several protesters lose eyes, dozens are killed. President Sebastián Piñera declares a state of emergency and on October 19th a curfew is declared in Santiago from 10pm to 7am.

One night, after curfew, a young cellist named Paula Advis takes her cello to her balcony and plays the tune of Victor Jara's "El Derecho de Vivir en Paz." It comes with no small risk. The army's orders demand literal silence from citizens. No loud sounds are to be made that don't come from soldiers or cops.

"Victor Jara was tortured and murdered, his music was almost forbidden," she tells CNN. "His music has a powerful meaning for the people, a meaning of struggle and power to the citizens."[17] Jara's story and music ensure his name is known well beyond Chile's borders. A dedicated communist, he was a key figure in the vibrant

17 Gianluca Mezzofiore, 'A soprano started singing out her window in defiance of a government-imposed curfew in Chile', *CNN* (8 November 2019), https://www.cnn.com/2019/11/08/americas/soprano-chile-curfew-intl-trnd-scli.

Nueva canción movement that emerged during the 1960s and 70s in Latin America and the Iberian peninsula. "El Derecho de Vivir en Paz" is a fair encapsulation of *Nueva canción*'s values. Written in 1971, the song – whose title literally translates to "The right to live in peace" – does more than merely call for peace in Vietnam, openly celebrating Ho Chi Minh and the anti-colonial insurgency in Indochina. Jara, along with most artists in his orbit and the virtual entirety of Chile's left, were enthusiastic supporters of Allende's Popular Unity government, as well as the movement for workers' control that spread during its rule. His violent death at the hands of Pinochet's coup-makers is the stuff of tragic legend.

Nueva canción wasn't merely a genre, but an organized network of artists and musicians. Victor Jara, Violeta Parra, Sergio Ortega, collectives and groups like Inti-Illimani and Quilapayún. These radical musicians worked together, shared their theories and ideas, thought through ways that their music could help a Chilean socialist vision flourish.

Toward that end, they experimented creatively. They incorporated pop and rock structures with indigenous and peasant music. Reaching both forward and back, they pushed forward the evolution of these sounds and genres while also bucking the influence of Yankee cultural imperialism. Inherent in this was the idea that a new historical trajectory might be emerging, not from the heart of empire but from the energies of the most oppressed on a continent long dominated by American designs.

Days after Paula Advis defies the silence, her childhood friend and opera soprano Ayleen Jovita Romero walks on to her cousin's balcony and begins to sing Jara's song. She too is disturbed by the enforced silence. "I came out on the balcony to sing for the people," says Romero.

When she is finished, neighbors cheer and applaud. Then, faintly, the song rises from other balconies, some singing, some playing guitar or accordion.

The curfew doesn't work. Protests continue. Unions declare a general strike. Police and the army definitively lose control of the situation. To listen to protesters, it sounds like a point of no return has been reached. Either Chile will break definitively from its past, or it will cease to exist. One sign that captures the spirit of the protests, and the long simmer of an unfinished history, reads simply: "Neoliberalism was born in Chile. Now it will die here."

On October 25th, one million people flood the streets of Santiago, bringing the capital to a standstill. Among them is a group of almost one thousand guitarists and singers playing "El Derecho." Several Chilean pop stars collaborate to record and release their own version of the song, though their version is also criticized for dulling the song's radical politics.[18]

The grand orchestra performance in Plaza Bernardo Leighton feels climactic. First, the massive throng of classical musicians plays Mozart's *Requiem*. Then their own version of "El Derecho," as banners are raised with the names of protesters killed. Then to "El Pueblo Unido Jamás Será Vencido." Like "El Derecho," this song emerged from *Nueva canción*, written and composed by Sergio Ortega and Quilapayún, though compared to Jara's song, "El Pueblo" is far more forceful. As its echoes across the quiet streets of Santiago denote, "El Derecho" is a kind of quiet promise of victory. "El Pueblo," by contrast, is what is sung when victory is nigh, less a promise than a confirmation. Performed by such a large,

18 Suzy Exposito, 'Chilean All-Stars Revamp Víctor Jara's Protest Anthem, 'El Derecho de Vivir en Paz'', *Rolling Stone* (28 October 2019), https://www.rollingstone.com/music/music-latin/chile-all-stars-victor-jara-protest-song-el-derecho-de-vivir-en-paz-904667/.

assembled orchestra, it sounds absolutely epic.

Naturally, the placement of more than 400 classically trained musicians could not be spontaneous. Still, according to writer Daniela Fugellie, organizers of what would come to be known as the Requiem por Chile collective were taken aback by the magnitude of the response. Particularly because of the longstanding association between classical music and the Pinochet regime. As María José Jiménez, one of the collective's organizers, was quoted as saying, "classical music has for too many years been captured by the economic elite, while historically it has been on the side of revolutions... We are going back to the origins of an art that was made for the people."[19]

True, Mozart was a defender of the French revolution, as was Beethoven and many other composers in the era of European revolution. Which means that as much as this performance was a redefinition of well-known *Nueva canción*, it was also a redefinition of classical music, and a reclamation of a revolutionary history that remains alive and in play. According to musicians and performers, the audience that watched and chanted with them were the best they had ever performed for, hugging each other and crying, asking them to come back.

Piñera did not step down, despite loud demands to do so. He was, however, forced to call an elected convention tasked with rewriting Chile's constitution. With this came the possibility that the protections of a privatized daily life and the inequality that comes with it might be written out. In December of 2021, Chile elected Gabriel Boric – a young, libertarian socialist member of the Chamber of Deputies affiliated with the far-left Social Convergence party – as its president. Left-wing parties,

[19] See Daniela Fugellie, 'Requiems por Chile', in *Instantáneas en la Marcha: Repertorio cultural de las movilizaciones en Chile*, ed. by Lucero de Vivanco and María Teresa Johansson (Santiago: Ediciones Universidad Alberto Hurtado, 2021).

including Boric's Social Convergence and the Communist Party of Chile, gained enough votes to form a government, though its mandate was razor thin.

The vision of a new Chile offered to the country by its Constitutional Convention a few months later was a sweeping one: the establishment of a national health service, the guarantee of the right to unionize and strike, the definition of education and housing as basic rights beyond the parameters of profit, a ban on mining the country's glaciers and other sweeping ecological protections, basic autonomies for indigenous communities and other racial minorities. In other words, the new constitution would have broken with key elements of Pinochet's neoliberal legacy and replaced it with a progressive, even radical future. Its defeat in a nationwide referendum illustrates the level of opposition to that future not just outside of Chile but from within the country too via its right and center. It is also further proof that, even when attempting to win change through the ballot box, democracy can never let its center of gravity be entirely sucked into the arena of bare and formal elections.

It would be easy to predict that a repeat of Allende is on the cards. And no doubt, the world's most powerful countries, including the United States, are less than thrilled that leftists continue to win elections in Latin America. But history, as we've seen, does not move in a predictable fashion. Particularly when there are those willing to give it a push, to look at their existence as potentially reclaimed right down to the most elemental, to the air and water we imbibe, to the time and space we occupy. The fact is, we have no idea what will happen in Chile. Or anywhere else. Events may yet take us back to the same bleak futurelessness we've already been acquainted with. Or they may ultimately prove to be ours, to do with what we wish, our creative energies brought to bear on them.

There is no song that can literally shake the walls of the city. There are, however, songs that spring from our ability to do so, that insistently reacquaint us with the endless reserve of alternative visions we can have for our lives, if only we give ourselves over to them. They are dangerous visions, living not just in our minds' eye but in our moving bodies, giving us a chance to redeem the defeats of the past and the futures defeated with them. These are futures synonymous with liberation. They are also, against all odds, still possible.

Part Five
Shake the City Playlist

The more progress was made on this book, the clearer it became that a full playlist was necessary. One can describe a song with all the flowery language they like, but at the end of the day Elvis Costello's observation holds true: "Writing about music is like dancing about architecture." Better, then, to simply encourage readers to hear what is being written about, compare it to the text, and make their own judgement. All of the songs can be easily searched and heard online. Most can be found on YouTube. For less well-known artists, you may have to search for their Bandcamp or Soundcloud pages. And yes, begrudgingly, there is Spotify.

Some of the songs included here appear simply because they have been mentioned in the text. Others are here to give readers more familiarity with genres or songs they might not be familiar with. Still others are necessary for more fully grasping the aesthetic and musical points made in the book.

For example, the Ramones' 'Judy Is a Punk' and Fela Kuti's 'Zombie' are next to each other because they exemplify an argument made in the book's first chapter about how the tensions between capitalism's universality and the particularities of geography and culture manifest in the differences and similarities of what Mark Abel calls "groove music." Whereas both songs – released the same year – are excellent examples of metronomic time, syncopation and back-beat, Kuti's 'Zombie' has a far more distinct and complex approach to deep metricality, with so many more instruments and interlocking rhythms layered in so as to structure the listener's attention.

Junior Kimbrough's 'Lonesome Road' is on here because Kimbrough's own delta blues guitar-playing style is highly layered and has its own way of displaying these key elements of groove music. It also possesses the kind of hypnotic darkness that was what attracted the attention of the surrealists, as mentioned in Part Two of the book. One note of clarification regarding Scott Joplin and Buddy Bolden. There are no known extant recordings of either artist playing their compositions. Only their sheet music survives. Therefore, in giving readers a sense of ragtime's sound – particularly regarding the blue note and multi-levelled meter – I've been left a bit wanting.

The most "faithful" recordings of Joplin's music are based on piano rolls, and therefore on a notation system that, as covered in Part Two, standardized Joplin's music into something more intelligible to European ears. Ultimately, I've decided not to recommend any of these recordings. 'Maple Leaf Rag' is a well-known enough song. In Bolden's case this is far easier, given that his contemporary Jelly Roll Morton made several recordings of Bolden's songs, and his tribute 'I Thought I Heard Buddy Bolden Say' is a reworking of Bolden's 'Funky Butt'.

One of Fred Ho's compositions, 'Gadzo', is also here to give people a sense of what he meant when writing about kreolization. Two examples of various kinds of electronic dance music are included so that readers can hear for themselves the often-subtle differences between, say, Chicago house (Frankie Knuckles), and drum and bass (LTJ Bukem). The music of Them Are Us Too is included to provide some sense of the kinds of artists who contributed to the arts and music scenes that gravitated to the former Ghost Ship. Them Are Us Too member Cash Askew died in the 2016 fire.

There are a few songs that won't be appearing here. Though I am happy and even enthusiastic to provide examples of vaporwave, I won't be providing examples of its fascist or far-right subsets. True, the internet is enemy territory, and will be a cesspool that provides a home in one way or another for fascist musicians whether or not I draw attention to them. But as a Jew and a communist, I cannot in good conscience boost the music of people who want me dead. When I write of fashwave's relative lack of depth, you can either take my word for it or search for it yourself. It's easy enough to find.

Playlist:

Pet Shop Boys - 'West End Girls'
Ramones - 'Judy is a Punk'
Fela Kuti - 'Zombie'
Junior Kimbrough - 'Lonesome Road'
Erik Satie - 'Musique d'ameublement' as played in three parts by Marius Constant and Ensemble Ars Nova
Algiers - 'Irony. Utility. Pretext'
Lil Reese feat. Lil Durk and Fredo Santana - 'Beef'
Fred Ho & the Afro Asian Music Ensemble - 'Gadzo'
Jelly Roll Morton - 'I thought I heard Buddy Bolden say'
Lee "Scratch" Perry - 'Black Panta'
Pink Floyd - 'Money'
Skepta - 'That's Not Me'
Lethal Bizzle - 'Pow! (Forward)'
LTJ Bukem - 'Watercolours'
Frankie Knuckles - 'Your Love'
Burial - 'Raver'
Martha and the Vandellas - 'Dancing in the Street'
Clipping. - 'Knees on the Ground'
Moor Mother - 'Creation Myth'
Janelle Monae feat. Wondaland - 'HELL YOU TALMBOUT'
Kendrick Lamar - 'Alright'
Giovanna Daffini - 'Bella Ciao'
Them Are Us Too - 'Us Now'
New Dreams Ltd. - 'Blue Earth'
Quilapayún - 'El Pueblo, Unido, Jamas Sera Vencido'
Victor Jara - 'El Derecho de Vivir en Paz'

Author biography

Alexander Billet is a writer and artist whose work concerns the overlap between creative expression, radical geography, and historical memory. His writing has appeared in *Los Angeles Review of Books, Jacobin, Salvage, In These Times, Radical Art Review, Historical Materialism blog, Protean, Real Life, Marx & Philosophy Review of Books, Chicago Review, Against the Current*, and other outlets. A member of the Locust Arts & Letters Collective, he helps edit its publications, Locust Review and Imago. He lives in Los Angeles with his partner and two useless cats. His blog is alexanderbillet.com.

www.ingramcontent.com/pod-product-compliance
Lightning Source LLC
Chambersburg PA
CBHW030302100526
44590CB00012B/482